JILL B[

But I Want to Stay With You...

SIMON & SCHUSTER

AUSTRALIA

First published in Australia in 1999 by
Simon & Schuster (Australia) Pty Limited
20 Barcoo Street, East Roseville NSW 2069

A Viacom Company
Sydney New York London Toronto Tokyo Singapore

National Library of Australia
Cataloguing-in-Publication data:

Burrett, Jill F.
But I want to stay with you : talking with children about
separation and divorce.

Includes index.
ISBN 0 7318 0749 9.

1. Communication in the family. 2. Parenting, Part-time.
3. Children of divorced parents. 4. Stepfamilies. I. Title.

306.874

Set in Sabon 11/16
Printed in Australia by Griffin

10 9 8 7 6 5 4 3 2 1

CONTENTS

PREFACE

All parents go through some personal turmoil about the effects separation will have on their children. Some say they would have left their relationships years ago if it weren't for their anxieties about them. Other parents, who feel abandoned by their partner, may show their concern for their children by closing ranks protectively, making it difficult to give the children the freedom they need to continue an important relationship with the parent who has nominally left the marriage.

Everyone who goes through a separation also experiences a period of instability and emotional unrest which can make it difficult to provide the support and security a child needs, at a time when the child most needs it. And yet all parents want more than ever what they think is best for their children, at a time when they themselves are not in the best position to give it. Further down the track, shared parenting arrangements inevitably give rise to various kinds of hiccups which can be tricky to deal with in the best way for children, even when parents feel they're getting on OK with being separated. Sharing your children after a separation is hard.

All children need emotional support from their parents, support which makes them feel valuable as individuals and which gives them the right balance of firm guidelines and safe opportunities for expression and experimentation.

You can do a lot to help your children have this essential ingredient for their healthy development by learning to enhance your family communication skills. You'll also significantly help their adjustment to family change caused by separation and its consequences.

This book aims to teach parents how to talk with and respond to their children about separation, divorce and all the family challenges that go with it, in a way that helps them. From the beginning of a separation, when you have to face telling your children about it, to the creation of stepfamilies, it takes you through common separation-related behaviour expressed by children and shows how you can most effectively respond to it so that their real needs are met. It helps you sort out which behaviours you need to worry about and which you don't, by linking children's social and emotional development generally with life in a family divided by a separation.

The underlying philosophy of this book is that children need to be helped not to carry a sense of responsibility themselves for their parents' break-up; that they should not have to place blame for it, or make choices in order to help with decisions which should be adult ones; and that they need emotional freedom from involvement in their parents' unresolved ongoing relationship problems, so they can enjoy continuing their own relationships with both of their parents, their new partners and new children in their parents' new families.

Whether you wanted the separation or not, if you can use the challenge of your new family situation to motivate you to refine your parenting skills, you'll be doing your children a great favour. Also, you'll have the comfort of knowing you really did do your best for them in difficult circumstances that you didn't exactly plan for, which will help you with the guilt, sadness and sensitivities you may go on feeling about their situation. It'll also help you feel that you are still able to be the responsible and caring parent you set out to be.

I am again grateful to the many people who have come to me over the years about their separation-related difficulties, the source of most of my knowledge of what separated families face. Their search for new and better ways to handle their children's behaviour is what inspired me this time to create a separated parents' communication guide. I am also grateful to my own children for providing me with day-to-day opportunities for checking the way I communicate as a parent myself, and for getting on happily and independently with their own lives so that I could make time to write this book.

JB 1999

CHAPTER 1

COMMUNICATING AND FAMILIES

Communication, in its broadest sense, is the most important activity of our daily lives, the lifeblood of all our connections with other people. Communicating with our children, and helping them communicate with us, is the very essence of family life. Being a parent, despite our lack of specific training for it, is the responsibility we undertake which has the most far-reaching, long-term consequences of anything we do.

All parents want to be able to communicate with their children effectively, and hope their children will in turn communicate openly and helpfully with them. But not everyone is naturally a good communicator, whatever their ambitions may be! Most of us don't attend much to the way we communicate unless we come up against a problem, or we're in training for a public-speaking job. In most situations we're spontaneous, expressing ourselves just as it comes, amidst the ongoing daily round of family life. And most parents, whether they admit it or not, spend far less time communicating with their children than they think they do, as so much family interaction takes place on the run as a succession of instructions, statements and questions which don't amount to real two-way conversations, but which we still think of as communicating.

We tend to think of our children's welfare and development in terms of caring for their physical health, their academic, artistic, sporting and social development. We seldom deliberately set aside time and resources for the emotional education of our children, because we think we're doing this as we go along, nor do we recognise how much communication styles determine this and therefore shape our children's self-esteem.

The healthy development of your child's self-esteem, which is wholly dependent on how you as a parent communicates within the family, is the single most important ingredient for the achievement of their potential, which, of course, is our most important parenting goal. This is quite awesome when you think about it!

Some descriptions and definitions

First, we're going to go back to basics. It's often worth taking a fresh look at something you take for granted. Revisiting what seems obvious can generate useful insights, and maybe some of what follows you won't have thought about much before. We're going to be talking throughout this book about communication in its widest sense, because everything that happens between people sends out a message of some kind and attracts a response of some kind. Even an apparent non-response to a message (for example, disinterest, preoccupation, vagueness, rudeness, indecision, deafness, sulking, etc.) really communicates something, depending on how the sender chooses to interpret the non-response and how the 'non-responder' is intending to be received. Everything that happens between people communicates something, whether or not words are used. Therefore, it's more than talking together, having conversations, it's about *everything* a person transmits.

A message, which, of course, can be verbal or non-verbal, has an apparent or literal face value, a surface *meaning*. It often also has a hidden agenda, an *underlying meaning*, depending on the sender's motives and their system of values, whether they recognise this or not. It also always has an *emotional component*, intended or otherwise, such as tone of voice, pace, volume, language style, gestures, postural mannerisms, and the feelings which come through with the words and/or actions. A message also has a *context*, the setting in which the communication is taking place, which itself has physical and emotional or 'feeling' elements to it.

You can see already there is ample room for accidental or deliberate mixed messages and misinterpretations leading to mismatched responses. The scope for communication to be confusing and frustrating is enormous. When relations are strained between parents, anxiety, hurt, frustration, resentment and anger further disrupt productive communication, and a state of chronic stalemate often sets in. No wonder the most frequently nominated cause of relationship breakdown is 'we just can't communicate'!

Efficient communication, where confusion is minimal and outcomes are mutually satisfying, is achieved when the following happens:

- The communication is clear and *authentic*, or congruent. You say unambiguously what you mean, and you address people attentively using direct eye contact. Your non-verbal signals match the content of your message, and your underlying feelings match that content. With children we often have to cover up our real feelings to protect them from certain truths, or from our own failings, trying our hardest to be patient when we're feeling irritated. Nevertheless, your children usually know when you're covering up crossness and when you're pretending to be happy. So technically we're often inconsistent with our children, because we rightly want to prevent them from feeling responsible for our own state of mind. We want to protect them from things that upset us, and we withhold truths about a lot of family goings-on because they compromise the values we're trying to instil in our children. When there's a separation we may do a lot of 'covering up' for our partners in our efforts to try to keep our children's regard for that parent positive.

- You *listen* effectively. This means listening accurately because you give your full attention, rather than responding hastily, or with something else on your mind, which we all often do. You take time to reflect back on what you think was said and what you think the feelings underlying the communication were, so there is opportunity for clarification, for correction or for the addition of more information. This is *active listening*, which is a powerful preventer of misunderstandings and contributes to the establishment of rapport or empathy between people: see below. Unfortunately, because our own feelings are so readily aroused by things people do and say, we often respond before we've really listened, basing our response on assumptions we make about the communication without pausing to check whether our assumptions are valid. This is how most arguments begin.

- You use *self-responsible language*. This shows you recognise the difference between your own and other people's feelings and responsibilities. If you say to someone, 'I do not like what you did', then you cannot (in theory at least!) be contradicted because your perception and what you've decided to think and feel about the behaviour is yours alone. The other person may suggest you haven't received all the information about their action or that you perceived it unclearly for one reason or another, and then the meaning can be renegotiated and clarified. But if you say, 'You have made me angry', you may well be contradicted with a 'No, I didn't!', because you've assumed there was a deliberate intention to enrage you, and you've placed responsibility for your feelings with someone else. *You* are responsible for your reactions to things. If you communicate this, then you give the other person the opportunity to evaluate and perhaps change their behaviour. Then they can consider whether to examine their style of expression and change it if, for instance, people react angrily when they speak in this way.

If you attribute responsibility for your feelings to the other person, you'll probably receive a defensive or contradictory response which then leads to a competition or argument. However, you are entitled to perceive the message quite differently from the way the other person perceives it.

Parents wanting to be attentive and protective often feel responsible for their children's feelings and experiences, and forget to allow them opportunities to explore their situation, think for themselves and learn to generate their own solutions. They impose their own ideas and attitudes, thinking they must always solve their children's issues or predicaments. Further examples of self-responsible communication, using 'I' language, are 'I would like you to tidy your room' rather than 'You should keep your room tidy', or 'I feel upset when you seem to ignore me' rather than 'You annoy me'.

- *Rapport* exists between people when they each allow the other to have their own feelings, opinions and standpoints regardless of their own. When you take time to show that you can identify with another's position — put yourself in their shoes as it were — you communicate *empathy*.

This is different from sympathy, which is an expression of regret, pity or compassion. When there is empathy, each person feels *validated* and understood. Communication therefore flows because it's experienced as mutually reinforcing, and a feeling of real relationship develops, which encourages future communication.

Where does our communication style come from?

The style of communication patterns we use has its origins in how we were spoken to and dealt with from birth by our own parents or caretakers. We tend to copy this style automatically, sometimes despite our best intentions. This is because the family is the training ground where every individual learns to communicate. When we become parents we almost unconsciously seem to deal with our children very much as we were dealt with by our own parents. You may have experienced realising, or being told, just after an exchange with your child that you sound just like your mother or father!

Everyone has their own unique style of communicating because everyone's family background is, of course, different. Our language and verbal style reflect our inherent value system, our attitudes and temperament, which are shaped by a complex mixture of those qualities we inherit and the impact on us of experiences both within and outside the family. You're sure to know people who seem to have a lot of negatives or cautions in their talking (the 'yes, but' style as distinct from the 'why not?', more positive, optimistic style); others who tend to be a bit closed to alternatives because they seem to see the world very much from their own point of view; others who always want to assert their point of view and dominate conversations, be the one who is right and have the last word on a topic; those who tend to want to talk about themselves; or very quiet types who don't talk much at all. The range of styles is literally endless.

Effective communication in families

Healthy family communication involves all the elements described above and some important extras. In a family there is a hierarchy, as the members of a family group are not equal. Your developing children are emotionally dependent on you, the parents who head the group; you therefore have a great deal of power to influence how the family communicates because of your senior position. The right amount of parental authority, an open-mindedness about your child's own position as separate to yours, and an awareness of how much you influence your child, is very important to get right. This is because parent–child communication is not between equals, as your children are dependent for their development on the kind of messages about them that you give out, and will unconsciously copy your way of communicating. Providing children in a family with a positive, nurturing and secure environment depends entirely on what and how you communicate together, so we'll look more closely at what we should be aiming for to achieve this:

- Communication should be honest and mostly congruent: see above. That is, what the people involved (especially you parents) think, feel and say match up. It's 'straight', without any confusing hidden agendas or mixed messages.

- You all enjoy each other's company most of the time, and don't just get together from a sense of obligation.

15

- You enjoy your role as a parent more than you feel restricted by it.

- Everyone says openly that they care for and support each other.

- Everyone is allowed and even encouraged to talk about their hopes, anxieties and triumphs as individuals.

- The usual atmosphere at home is positive and the family language reflects this.

- Everyone is valued for who they are as an individual and encouraged to develop their own views and independence.

- You know when it's appropriate to make decisions for your children — although you always listen to them — and when it is appropriate to give them choices.

Most of you will probably agree with the above in theory, though you may feel your family falls short of the ideals the list reflects, especially when you're trying to negotiate a separation. As we've mentioned, many of us are unaware of how we really project ourselves, because we're just busy doing the best we can in our own way. But we may have all sorts of attitudes, stresses and other sensitivities on our minds which colour how we come across to people, without realising they are there, let alone intending them to come through.

There may also be inconsistencies between how you'd like to see yourself, what you believe in, what you declare about your priorities and values, what you want to project to others, particularly your children, *and how you actually behave!* These inconsistencies are communicated to others, causing resentment and misunderstandings. Relationship breakdown itself involves a major inconsistency, as you are having to abandon your ideals for a happy and united family life and inflict a disappointment on your children, which is a major compromise of your initial values.

Negotiating a separation involves many other kinds of inconsistencies which are usually perceived very differently by each parent. For example, a common grievance arises when a father declares his love for and commitment to his children, but is never there for them as far as the wife and mother is concerned. She feels his actions contradict his professed values, and finds it difficult to support his efforts to negotiate having time with the children after separation.

We've all been guilty sometimes of snapping at someone who isn't really the correct target for our irritability. This often happens with children, who, because of the urgency of many of their communications, frequently don't choose the right moment to be demanding, and elicit a short response from parents with other things on their minds. How often have you chosen a quiet moment when the children seem settled to make that important telephone call, only to find that your four-year-old immediately rushes up wanting your urgent attention?

Children are constant, demanding, self-centred and irritating sometimes, as well as being inspiring and enjoyable at others. Parents are human too and everyone lets themself and their children down sometimes! As parents we may find ourselves using a lot of limiting, commanding statements, such as 'don't touch', 'don't do that', with our children.

Of course, these are often necessary for the safety of young children, but they are negative in the sense that they are prohibiting. We sometimes find ourselves saying things such as 'You must try harder' or 'You took John's toy', statements which are accusing, if sometimes deserved. We also often use 'should statements', which imply something has been done wrongly and the child is not as capable, or obliging, as they 'should' be.

All these styles may seem necessary sometimes, but they tend to disregard children's feelings and attitudes, and to prescribe how they ought to be in terms of what you want or think they should be. You have such power in how you talk to your children! Effective limit-setting is a very important part of parenting, but we all need to look at how we do it and how we affect our children — whether we help them or inhibit them — and we shall be looking at this further in Chapter 6.

How do you rate yourself as a communicator?

Take a look at a recent family scenario and make an honest assessment of your contribution. How much do you use blaming, fault-finding, teasing, humiliating, belittling, sarcasm, put-downs, harassing, nagging, focussing on omissions or failures rather than achievements, imposing your own standards, etc.? We're all guilty of these negatives sometimes. How much do you listen, inquire, show understanding of your child's position, give praise, invite solutions, etc.? The ability to recognise and take into account another's position in your expressions is an essential ingredient for effective communication, as we've seen.

How often do you assert your point of view clearly with people at the time you are speaking to them, or end up thinking after the conversation that you didn't say what you really felt at all? How often do you find you have a point of view but you usually give in, just to keep the peace? How often do you need to win people round to your point of view in order to feel comfortable and confident about your opinion? Do you need other people's approval in order to feel secure about your own opinions? How well does the content of your verbal messages match up with your non-verbal signals such as postural gestures and emotional tone? Do you often talk to people while doing something else? Do you look people in the eye when you're talking to them, or avert your gaze while finding your words, or when you feel anxious, for example? Are you unsettled by periods of silence and find you keep talking to fill in pauses? Do you find you instantly want to reply to people, perhaps defensively, even interrupt them before they're finished, or do you pause and ask for clarification or further information before you respond? What do people whose opinion you respect tend to think about how you communicate?

The answers to all these kinds of questions will give you some insights into how you come across to people, how well people are likely to understand you, how clearly you communicate, and how satisfied your conversations leave you feeling.

Now we're going to start thinking about actual family life and consider some general ideas about things you can *do* with and *say* to your children which will help you all to relate well together.

Getting on with children

Some people, whether they are parents or not, just seem to have a knack with kids, naturally attracting their interest and admiration. Most of us would like to have children classify us as 'ace', 'cool', 'excellent', 'brilliant', or some current buzz word for favoured people, wouldn't we? Everyone likes to be liked. We're glad when we hear our child tell us about an adult, perhaps one of their teachers, that they really like and we're interested in the reasons why. Here are some things that lead to happy and mutually reinforcing relations with children:

- Spending time with your children makes them feel important to you. Be willing to stop what you're doing entirely, get 'on the floor' with them, and give them your undivided attention over something quite simple. If you're the kind of parent who's only prepared to be with children when you are doing the things *you* like, think what this can communicate to them — they're not important enough for you to get down to their level, and what they want to do isn't interesting to you. Stop what you're doing when your teenager wants to talk to you about something important and give them your undivided attention.

- Be prepared really to play with your children. Join in as an equal, not always as someone with superior knowledge and experience; even pretend you need them to show you how to do things. Be abandoned and spontaneous sometimes, so you're momentarily laughable, forgetting about age gaps for a while. Children love this being silly together. Make time to have this kind of fun sometimes!

- Don't forget how, even in our 'high-tech', 'screen-play' age, our children can be entertained simply without any machinery when they're getting all the attention of a valued caretaker. This often allows time for building real trusting communication into a relationship. Children then see you're not always preoccupied with your own tasks and interests, happy when they're out of the way and being amused by someone or something else. Showing you find them worth spending time with tells them you think they are important to you.

- Sometimes you'll be inconvenienced by your children not being able to amuse themselves independently. Children learn to do this from you and their teachers. They need to learn the joy of discovery and the value of perseverance, an important part of learning to be independent. Have plenty of ideas up your sleeve which you're willing to spend some time introducing them to. Involve them in helping you with your hobbies and interests even though their input may not always be convenient or give quite the results you want!

- When you must disapprove of something or demand obedience, make sure you try to do it in a way which doesn't convey disrespect or dislike for your child personally. When you're cross it's easy to say things which are put-downs, such as 'You're so stupid' or 'How come Tom can always find his shoes and you never can?'. Avoid comparisons with other children, especially brothers and sisters. Steer clear of making over-generalisations about their behaviour, creating expectations which will tend to be lived up to ('Dad says I'm stupid, so I must be'). Examine your language, and make sure your message says that it's their behaviour, not them, that's unacceptable. Exercising authority need not be demeaning or undermining. Look at how often you find yourself issuing restraints. Can you cut out some of the negative content of your exchanges? For example, younger children naturally dawdle, so are you leaving enough time to get them organised? Can you minimise confrontations by putting at least some of the things you can't allow them to fiddle with out of their range? Try not to get irritated and impatient so that they feel they regularly exasperate you.

- Don't forget to explain things to children. They are inexperienced, and everything in their lives has to be learned at some stage. You may be looking for more than they are yet capable of. Show respect for their position and tell them what you expect of them, or you may get frustrated when they won't (perhaps because they can't) cooperate, or they make a mess of things. Try to make them keen to try things, not afraid of disappointing you. You're working on building a relationship which guides your child onwards with a continuing sense of achievement.

- Don't give young children too much choice about things in an effort to treat them with respect. They'd often rather not have to think too hard about what to have for breakfast, or what to wear, for example. And definitely don't give them a choice when you have a preference yourself which you intend to insist on; this happens surprisingly often without parents realising they're doing it. Listen to yourself.

- Children don't necessarily know what they think and feel about things (neither do a lot of adults for that matter!); nor do they express themselves in an organised or consistent way all the time. A lot of what you hear will not seem very logical, because it's spontaneous, momentary and random. They often say things just for impact, to excite, provoke,disturb, annoy, express anger and to manipulate. Try not to let this sort of thing get to you personally so you feel you must be failing somewhere. A certain amount of it is normal. They're busy learning what they think and feel about themselves and the world, what reactions their behaviour attracts and about what limits will be set. You don't need to react literally to everything they say or do but you should definitely set limits on destructive, hurtful and rude talk unless they're very obviously play-acting.

- Children aren't naturally forthcoming once a moment has passed; they move on to the next event or feeling quickly. As a result they may appear unenthusiastic, even secretive. Don't insist that they discuss something with you; try to sound interested but not pushy. They'll tell you things as and when they want you to know.

- When your child brings you some emotional communication, try to become aware of what it is. Recognise the emotion as an opportunity for closeness and teaching. Listen sympathetically, giving permission for them to have their feelings. Help them find words to label the emotion they are experiencing, and try to help them work out a solution with you. Many parents feel they must solve their children's predicaments for them, as we mentioned earlier. If you listen attentively, inviting them to talk, responding to the emotions uncritically, you'll be helping your child work out their own solutions with your support; this is much more useful to them, because it enhances their sense of self-worth and independence. We'll be talking more about emotional expression in Chapter 7, although feelings are, of course, present in all communications.

Communication and family change

Families undergo many stresses, and how you communicate in your family will determine how well you weather them. Separation and its consequences are major ones. We mentioned above how all the emotions of separating can affect your communication style. Communicating effectively about major changes in the family make-up and their ongoing consequences will help you all to adjust. Sometimes you'll be caught on the hop with something your child says or does which seems to be about some aspect of your separation, and you'll stumble for the right response, do your best to say or do something helpful without letting your own adult feelings of guilt, sadness or anger come through too much. Later you may be left wondering whether you handled your child the best way. The moment might have passed by, but there will be plenty more similar ones to come, which you can prepare for.

So if you haven't thought to examine yourself as a communicator, now's the time to take a long hard look and, by learning new ways of handling your children's expressions about their separated family, make an active and responsible contribution to helping your divorce and your new kind of family life be less negative and troublesome than it need be. If parents can relate to their children in a way which is accepting of the contributions of everyone to the family, past and present, then communication will be more likely to remain open and productive all round.

In any family, but particularly one when there has been a separation, good communication is important for children's security. You need to have the right amount of honesty about what's gone on in the family without being too much of a martyr or a blame-placer, which inhibits their freedom to enjoy relations with important people. Being too protectively secretive about real events and human failings, which we often want to shield them from, can make them confused and anxious. This is because your communications will be inconsistent with real events and feelings, and they probably know or suspect more than you think they do. You need to find the right balance between how much of your own feelings to communicate to them, so that you come across as authentic and congruent, and how much to hide from them because your feelings are so often about their other parent's dealings with you. Children need the right amount of openness about real events and feelings to maintain useful and respectful relationships with both of their parents despite family disappointments. This will mean that everyone's adjustment to changing circumstances, where belonging to two households and having multiple family relationships is going to be the norm, will be much, much easier.

In the chapters that follow we'll take family communication and apply the principles of relating effectively with children to common separation-related scenarios, and show how you can help your children with the challenges they face; we'll give suggested responses, explaining why they help; interpret common emotional blockages and unhelpful attitudes in parents which interfere with how we deal with our children; and we'll explain how children commonly react to separation situations to help you understand their behaviour. You'll be able to finetune the suggested responses to suit the ages of your own children and similar situations you've experienced in your family. And if you find you become intrigued by this important business of communicating, because, of course, it has applications for all walks of life, you'll find some further reading suggestions. You can make your divorce into a valuable personal growth opportunity!

CHAPTER 2

BREAKING THE NEWS

Habitual patterns of communicating in your family will, of course, have been established well before the possibility of a separation arose. How successfully you manage your separation as far as your children are concerned depends on how you communicate with them about it, and this begins with preparing them for a significant family event that wasn't really what either of you had in mind. Breaking disappointing news is very hard for any parent.

Everyone's separation is different. Therefore, children (and their remarks and reactions) will be affected by such things as how mutual the decision was and how jointly it has been faced by their parents, whether there's a third party involved, how much open conflict there's been for how long, etc.

Leading up to the time when you've got to tell the children, or one of you is starting to insist that you take this step, there may be a period of several months when there's tension and uncertainty 'in the air', however hard you're trying to conceal it from them. Children will deal with this in a variety of ways according to their age, temperament and what they feel is expected of them. They may be apparently oblivious to it; they may internalise it; or their behaviour may change in uncharacteristic ways (they may be, for example, moody, clingy, attention-seeking, aggressive). They may ask you what the matter is when they can sense you're upset, tense or preoccupied.

What you say to them about what's going on is very important at this time. Marriages sometimes take ages to progress from being unsatisfactory to being so bad that someone does something about it. Children sense unhappiness in their parents very acutely, and can feel very insecure if this period of uncertainty goes on and on. Many parents put off saying anything to their children for fear of putting them through a bad experience when there may still be a chance things will work out. It's much better for them if you say something, even if it has to be a bit open-ended and uncertain. And if it's going to happen, or one of you is sure it is, don't spend too many months avoiding the upsetting business of telling the children and of course, don't avoid it altogether!

If you were to get back together successfully, it would take some getting used to by the children after adjusting to your separation, and this is understandable, but most children would welcome a reconciliation. Don't let thinking you might work things out deter you from saying anything for months and months.

'My wife and I haven't been happy for a while. When she gets upset after we've been having a discussion, she gets very emotional. The other day my eight-year-old daughter asked me what Mum was so upset about lately. How should I have answered her? Should she know at her age that we're having marital troubles?'

Depending on your style of interacting with your kids, you can do a number of things. Don't feel you have to pretend everyone's fine. Your daughter is sensing that her mum isn't, and it's best to explain it somehow rather than gloss over it, and have her invent her own explanation and worry privately, perhaps that it's her fault. Children should know that Mum and Dad don't agree on everything. Parental consistency is a bit of a myth even in very happy marriages.

You could be proactive and gather your children together, and say something such as: 'Mum and I are having a few problems, but they're between us and nothing to do with anything you've done, so try not to worry too much. People don't always see eye-to-eye on things, even though they love each other, and sometimes they have differences that are hard to resolve. We're trying our hardest to work it out, but sometimes it's upsetting and we might show it, but we're OK'. Or say something along these lines which doesn't skirt around the reality that things are happening, but also doesn't place blame. Such a statement reassures children that it's not their fault, that interpersonal tension is part of life, and it tells them you know that how you are does affect them. It sets a proper boundary between what is parent business and what is child business and this enhances their sense of security.

Encourage your wife to be part of the discussion and reassure her she is not failing as a parent if she reveals her feelings to the children. If you try to imagine what it would be like for your children to hear it straight that their parents are having marriage problems and you think this would be awful and upsetting for them, yes, you're probably right. But it's worse for them if neither of you says anything, you pretend it's not happening, and your communication is incongruent with the emotional reality that they're well aware of. They won't be able to approach you about it if you are in effect conveying that it's an unmentionable subject.

As things progress, if you get asked what will happen if you can't work it out, you'll probably feel anxious about letting them in on the possibility that you may split up. You love them and you know this will destabilise them.

'I was really uncomfortable when my daughter (ten years old) asked, 'Mummy, are you going to get divorced?'. I found I said 'No' out of fear, when I knew that that was where we were rapidly heading. Was I wrong to lie?'

You could only do what you did at the time, so don't be too hard on yourself; no parent likes to disappoint or distress their child. There are two options for you now. You could talk to her soon and say that your 'No' really meant you very much hope it isn't going to happen. Spend some time with her explaining that sometimes things between mums and dads can be fixed and sometimes they can't; that you've been trying really hard to find a way for things to work out; and that whatever happens both her parents love her very much but there may have to be some changes. You could refer to someone you know whose family has split up and how they seem to be getting along OK. Your child is sure to know all about divorce from television shows and celebrity media coverage!

Alternatively, you could leave things until you and her father are ready to tell her that it's definite. Don't worry about technically having lied in answer to her question. The truth when it comes to relationship matters has very many shades of grey. Your 'No' probably reassured her at the time and communicated to her that you hoped you wouldn't be getting divorced, which is probably true. She's unlikely to come back and say, 'But you promised me you weren't going to, Mum!', and if she does you can explain that you were confused and upset about it all, you were still desperately hoping you wouldn't at that time, but things have changed now. You needn't say that you really knew you were probably divorcing at the time she asked you.

'My husband recently announced he was leaving me for another woman. I'm hurt and angry, of course, and I don't know how to tell the children. I can't talk to him right now and I'm scared of what they'll think if they find out about her.'

Obviously it's going to be very difficult if the decision to divorce is far from mutual, as sadly it so often is. A unilateral decision to leave has been announced, leaving you feeling rejected and abandoned. It's probably better that you do tell your children, preferably together, that Dad is leaving and he has found someone new, unless you can agree together to keep the fact of the other person from the children until later. Sometimes it surprises parents that children are more comfortable if there is an apparent reason for a separation, especially if there has been a civilised, conflict-free estrangement going on at home. It makes more sense to them. However, it obviously places the blame for the break-up very much on the parent who has a new rival friendship. Try to let your children know that although you are hurt and upset, you'll get used to it in time (even if you feel hopeless now). They shouldn't have to worry too much about whether you'll be all right, feeling they have to look after you and needing to blame their dad for doing this to you. (They *will* blame him and be angry with him and he will have to try to help them with this.) Remember about asserting the right reassuring boundaries between adult business and child business.

If you can talk this through together as a couple so much the better, although right now talking together is understandably difficult. If you really can't talk together, you should somehow tell him — in writing perhaps — that you're going to tell the children so they can understand better why you're upset. Once they know, if he doesn't know they know, and he doesn't mention it, they'll feel uncomfortable, and more likely to align themselves with you because there seem to be important secrets within the family. This will just make it worse for them. If their father knows they know, he can take responsibility for how he then communicates with them about what has happened.

Even though the decision can't be changed, it'll help you preserve some mutual respect if you can both try to come to some understanding together, perhaps with the help of a properly qualified counsellor, of how your relationship got to where it is now.

If you can talk to your children with confidence and compassion, acknowledging responsibility without blame, with lots of reassurances of your continued love for them, and give them some idea of how the future will work out (at least in the short term), then you'll be doing OK. Recognise that telling the children is going to be hard for both of you in different ways.

'How much should you tell children of five and seven years old about why you're separating?'

The best approach does depend on the ages of your children of course, and also on how you're getting on as a couple at this difficult time and the particular circumstances leading up to the separation. Prepare yourself first: ask yourself what you want them to know, then check what it's appropriate for them to know given their ages and emotional maturity. Try to be confident that you know your children best and can work out what they can handle. Don't feel you've got to give them too much detail; they can't possibly understand what's gone on and, if you're honest, you probably can't either!

They'll be satisfied, to begin with anyway, with less detail than you think you need to give. Remember, the real truth as you see it, which will be different from your spouse's version, may put you or their other parent in a bad light, which undermines them personally because their sense of identity emanates equally from both of you. It's surprising how often parents don't think about this, so remember it whenever you feel tempted to let out something really nasty about your partner. Certain truths cannot be concealed. Try to discuss them as events that have happened, without making explicit judgments, describing them as difficult and disappointing aspects of human nature that are hard to deal with. You'll be tempted to avoid mentioning some things, but think about how mystifying it must be for children to have their parents covering up things that they know about.

'Should we talk to the children together? We're disagreeing about how our separation should be explained and we don't trust each other to be fair in what we say. Won't it be harder for them to see us talking about it together?'

Keep trying to talk together as a couple about timing and content and who's going to say what. Perhaps you need to give yourselves some more time for preparing to talk together as a family. If you'd rather do it separately because you're worried about the emotional discomfort, that's OK, but consider that certain emotions will be appropriate for the occasion, and you can help your children by acknowledging them and letting them be felt. (Remember the value of congruence between what you say and the feelings that go with it, discussed in Chapter 1.) Doing it together affirms to the children, right from the start of your new kind of family, that matters which concern them directly are still your joint responsibility. This gives them a reassuring show of solidarity, which is a very good start to a separation.

However, destroyed trust does go with break-ups and you may find you aren't ever going to agree on how to explain things. Try nevertheless to agree that you can each give a version of your point of view, acknowledging that the way you each see it is very different. For example, you might say: 'Dad has decided he isn't happy and he wants us to separate. I'm very sad about this as I'd like to work things out between us, because I think we can. But Dad doesn't and we all have to try to accept that we see things very differently, and get on as best we can without thinking one of us is most at fault. Marriages are often hard [etc.]'. The father could say something like: 'I haven't been happy for some time now, and I've made the decision to separate from Mum, which means I'm going to move out soon. I know my decision has hurt Mum a lot and that is difficult for you. I'd expect you to be angry and upset with me too. But I haven't decided to leave *you*, although it might seem like that, and I'm looking forward to working out how we'll be spending time together, which Mum and I will talk about together as soon as she feels up to planning it with me'. Follow this with all the reassurances about you being unhappy not being in any way their fault. This is straight talking about what's happened and is much less mystifying for children than trying to gloss over the truth to protect them from their parents' failings, which we often want to do. Also, it gives children permission to feel things about their parents that fit with what's happened.

'How soon before their father moves out should we tell them we're separating?'

It can be a good idea to have some time together as a family, despite strained feelings, before either of you walks out the door, to allow the announcement to sink in, questions to be asked, feelings to be expressed and reassurances given. The very sudden departure of a parent can feel more like an act of abandonment, and children can be uncertain to begin with as to how to 'reach' that parent, or they may be so angry or self-blaming that they want to cut themselves off from them. Time together allows them to get used to the idea, have conversations, and think about what spending time with their separated parents is going to be like. You can get used to the experience of spending separate time with your children, while still at the same address.

This can make seeing your children from a new home base when you do move a little less strange. Try to have a rough idea of how, when and where they're going to see you already worked out so they can start to envisage it. Helping to find the new accommodation together can be reassuring.

'We got together as a family to announce our decision to separate. We thought we'd see what the children's reactions were before deciding who was going to live where, and see what they had to say about it. My eight-year-old said he wanted to live with his father, and his sister, who's ten years old, said, 'Good, I'll stay with Mum!'. (They argue quite a lot.) We didn't know what to say. Their fourteen-year-old brother announced that he was going to see where we were moving to before he decided because he wants to live near the beach. Rick (their father) thinks they should choose, but I'm not sure what's best.'

However liberal you are about wanting to give your children choices, this one is a very different kind of issue. You sound as if you have faced your separation reasonably jointly, but even so, you both need to consider the position you will put your children in if you ask them to choose between their two parents. Unless you have agreed to share their time with each of you in the future equally, with both households to be just as much their 'home', then living with one of you will feel like a choice in favour of that parent at the expense of the other, and this is too hard for them. Also, they can't possibly know what the separation is going to be like until it's started. *You* should make the decision for them and put it in place, at least to begin with. Older children may, of course, want to have more of a say, but even then there may be all sorts of reasons behind their apparent preferences which don't necessarily reflect what's best for them.

You'd surely agree that a brother and sister shouldn't choose to live apart because they argue! What you as parents can agree on is probably going to be what's best for them anyway, because it's more likely to be an arrangement that you can both support. It will prevent them feeling they've made difficult choices they feel responsible for and have to live with, which should properly be made for them by their parents. Try to talk to Rick, and tell the children you're going to do this and then you'll get back to them about it. If everything remains friendly and flexible there's no reason why they should all stay together necessarily. Perhaps you and Rick could go to see a professional for some advice if you find you can't decide.

'I was getting anxious that if we left it much longer the children might hear from somewhere else that we were having problems. I knew we had to do it but I was dreading it because I felt the whole thing was my fault. Sam's eighth birthday was coming up in a few days and I didn't want to spoil it. I must say that I was full of doubts about when the right moment was going to be. I hope I timed it OK and didn't ruin his birthday for him.'

You're right, there's never a perfect moment and we all put off difficult tasks. You probably didn't ruin his birthday and it gave you a good opportunity straight away to show that many family events will go on just as usual. The courage you showed in telling him despite your doubts and anxieties would have communicated your concern for him to know what's going on and may have explained some of the tension or unhappiness he had noticed. All these are important messages for him.

Timing, and therefore content, may not be all that well planned when it comes to it, because one of you leaves suddenly and emotionally, or you're putting it off because you know it's going to be difficult. You'll just have to do the best you can to give some kind of explanation that reassures the children and isn't too critical of anyone. As we've explained, there are advantages to doing it together as a family, but choose an unhurried time, not when someone's got to rush off to soccer practice!

'I was caught unawares the other day when my fourteen-year-old son told me his mother had said she'd announced we were separating. I was a bit cross because I felt she'd jumped the gun, putting me in an awkward position with my own son, and I didn't know what to say. I mumbled something about still hoping to work it out, but he could tell I was awkward and embarrassed. What should I do?'

When you haven't planned what to say to the children, and you find out that your partner has already spoken to them, prepare yourself to say something soon. Then work out why you think you're separating and acknowledge that the reasons may be confused or hurtful to you. Have a chat with your son soon. With a fourteen-year-old you can say that you didn't handle it too well when he mentioned it, and explain why with a comment like 'I hadn't realised Mum had decided to mention it, and we hadn't communicated with each other about how to break the news'. Ask him what he feels about it and you may learn about what his mum said (or rather, what he thinks she said!) if you haven't been able to ask her yourself. Appreciate that he felt able to approach you about it. Be willing to acknowledge to him that you and his mum don't agree on why things have turned out this way, and that your respective perceptions of the marriage are obviously quite different.

This should prevent any 'but Mum said it was because…' replies which are the beginnings of a search for who to blame. So be one step ahead and communicate in this way so that your different views are not in competition. He'll be comforted by hearing something from you but will be more awkward with you if you've said nothing. He may make up something that's way out, and may feel he isn't supposed to mention it. He probably needs to.

'My daughter has hardly spoken to me since we told her we were separating. Over the last few months her father has been bending over backwards to endear himself to all the children. He's been spending much more time with them than he ever did before. I'm wondering what he's been saying to them about us separating. Sarah has been quite rude to me. The other day she announced she wanted to live with him, even though we've agreed on the future arrangements. How can I break her silence?'

After they've been told, children need time to get used to the news and may react by withdrawing or appearing to have taken sides. You should try to see some good in the children spending more time with their father. He is probably anxious about losing touch with them once you're living separately and wants to reassure them that he cares for them. Try not to be put off by your daughter's silence. Choose your moment and tell her you want to say a few things to her, that you realise she may not want to say anything, but you want her to hear them anyway. Acknowledge that it's a difficult time for everyone and you hope she'll come round to accepting your part in it. Remind her that the arrangements for the future have been agreed on, and will stay as they are, but that you and her father are interested in her views about them. She probably wants to go on living with both of you and feels that in the future she may lose out on her father's recently renewed attention, or she may be worried about how he'll get along on his own. Her silence may be her way of expressing her anger about what's happened. Tell her it's OK if she feels angry with you, that you understand, but that you'd prefer she talked with you and hope she'll feel ready to soon. Then leave it for a while and try to get on with ordinary family life for the time being.

Choosing your lines

How you tell your children about your separation is so important that we're going to give you some more suggestions for suitable lines to say:

- 'We can't find a way to be happy together, we've really tried to solve our differences, but very sadly we've had to decide we can't live together anymore.'

- 'It's going to be difficult for you to understand and in many ways I'm not sure I entirely understand it, so maybe don't expect it to make sense.'

- 'Sometimes we'll all be sad and angry that this has had to happen, but we've each in our own way thought about it long and hard and this is the only solution.'

- 'We still want to be very much a family but it'll be a different kind of one from now on.'

- 'You'll still see lots of both of us, but separately.'

- 'We may disagree on lots of things, but there'll always be one thing we share with lots of love and care, and that's you.'

- 'Nothing you could've done would have prevented our decision so it certainly isn't your fault.'

- 'We'll all be a bit unsettled for a while as we get used to it, but let's get on with things the best we can.'

- 'Good things may come out of this like us being able to spend more time together once we reorganise ourselves.'

- 'Yes, you may think I've been hurtful or uncaring at times, said and done things I'm not proud of as we've tried to work things out, and I'm sorry for my part in upsetting you and Mum/Dad.'

- 'And, yes, it's true I don't want this to happen but I accept that if both of us can't be happy, one of us wanting to stay together isn't going to work, however much I might want it to.'

- 'You're bound to have noticed a bit of tension lately and now it's time for us to let you know we've been having problems we can't find a way to sort out, and so we're separating because it'll be for the best.'

- 'Yes, it's true that we don't both want to separate, so Mum's pretty upset, and I most likely seem to blame for upsetting her and leaving you. This makes it pretty hard for all of us but we'll get through it, so try to think of it as our problem not yours if you can because neither of us wants you to worry about it too much.'

- 'Maybe what I'm saying mightn't seem to fit with what you've heard from Dad, but we often see things differently and it's not that one of us is right and the other wrong.'

Some of these suggested sayings may seem impossible to come up with in the heat of the moment. However, consider them because they're designed to help children feel involved and informed but not in a way that makes them believe they are responsible. The sayings also: give information but not so much that children are confused; convey that it's not a decision that's been made lightly, because you know it's important and they'd rather it wasn't happening; are designed to convey from the outset that neither the children nor Mum/Dad is deficient or otherwise blameworthy (though you may be quite sure your partner is!); show that there's a plan for the short-term future to reassure them that family life is going to continue just as usual in many respects; and explain that a certain amount of upset feelings will be involved, but that these can be managed. You can tailor-make a suitable approach according to the age make-up of your family and your separation circumstances. We'll talk more about how to deal with children's questions about who's responsible for the separation when we consider blame in Chapter 7.

Key Points for Telling Children You're Separating

- Recognise that breaking the news is always hard because of the anxieties you both have about what you're doing to the children. But don't put it off too long once it's inevitable, or avoid addressing it altogether.

- Don't make the mistake of trying to hide your relationship doubts and problems completely from your children. If you announce that you're separating, they may feel unable to understand why you have to if you've managed to coexist all right so far, and angry that you can't continue to do so. Communicating openly in families about ideals and failings is useful, especially when it comes to separating. Children may wonder what they've done to deserve being in a family that hasn't worked if you've been too idealistic and evasive about the realities of relationships and families, and haven't prepared them with some information about what's going on, or if you avoid addressing them responsibly about separating.

- Do it as a complete family if you can, and allow emotional expression appropriate for the occasion. If you can't, don't leave it to just one of you. Each of you should address your children in your own carefully thought-out way.

- If your children are of widely differing ages you may find it works better to address them one by one, as well as in a family group.

- Don't put off telling the children because you haven't agreed on a shared parenting plan. Say that you and Mum/Dad are working hard on finalising some arrangements to get started with.

- Try not to convey to your children that separation is catastrophic because it is devastating to you. This can be a tall order, of course. Tell them that life is full of challenges of various kinds, and though this is a big one, you'll all come through it OK in the end. In other words, you're expressing your confidence in them, while not making light of the news; giving them an important message about life; and recognising that their feelings about it may be different from yours. It may not, in fact, be as catastrophic for them as you fear.

- If you get a very emotional response from your child, try to show you recognise and accept their feelings, rather than telling them not to be angry or not to cry. Try to be supportive about their other parent even if you resent them, by saying the decision will hopefully be the right one in the end even if it isn't what you want right now. However cross or resentful you are inside, you're trying to convey to your children that you'll cope (they won't have to prop you up) and that their mum hasn't destroyed their father, (and is therefore to blame) or vice versa.

- To help you avoid being too judgmental or blaming in your explanations, use self-responsible 'I' language: see Chapter 1. For example, instead of saying, 'He hurt me very badly', say, 'I feel very hurt about what he did'; and instead of saying, 'She's upset me a lot', say, 'I feel very upset about Mum's actions'. Remember that you own your responses to events and you cannot accurately assume people's intentions.

- Communicate to your children that they can bring up any questions or concerns with you at any time, and be prepared to listen to them attentively and reassuringly.

CHAPTER 3

BELONGING TO TWO HOUSEHOLDS

Your separation has begun and so have your careers as separated co-parents. The first few weeks or months may be uneasy as everyone gets used to this new way of being a family, in fact, two families. Your apprehension as parents is often compounded by your efforts at personal recovery from the disappointment and frustrations of your failed partnership. Your children need you to be positive and confident about everything that concerns them, without you glossing over or making too much of the real difficulties that are involved, or inhibiting their freedom to make the necessary adjustments by transmitting to them your hurt, resentment, anxiety or anger. You both have to try to give positive encouragement about their time with each of you. This is always hard when your feelings about the break-up are difficult to cope with.

Hopefully, you've been able to tell the children how they're going to maintain contact with both their mum and dad, particularly if they're living mainly with one of you and the other has moved away and set up a new place where they are going to spend time regularly. However well you've applied the principles of the previous chapter, your children may be uncertain about the future; they may get caught up in worrying about pleasing both their parents; they may feel your separation is somehow their fault; they may yearn for you to reconcile; and they may find the transition between being in the care of one parent and the other uncomfortable, because it focuses on the reality that their mum and dad really are separated now. They may express these feelings in various ways which are not always easy to understand or deal with and which require sensitive and reassuring responses from parents.

'Sometimes lately my two girls (seven and eleven years old) say they don't want to spend the weekend with their father. They don't say why. Should I force them to go?'

Uncertainty or reticence about arranged time with a parent, or even refusal to go, is quite common early on in the first few months after separating, and even later on when other commitments clash with arranged periods of contact, or major changes occur like the arrival of new partners.

If you have a reasonably friendly agreement that your children spend time regularly with their father you should try to keep it up despite their occasional apparent disinterest or apprehension. *You* may not want to have anything to do with him but they should, of course, be helped to do so. First, try all the techniques you've learned to use over the years when you've had to coax your children into doing something they're showing reluctance about. Reassure them in all the ways you do when you have to make them do something they're saying they don't want to do, like go to school, visit relations, write a thank-you letter, go to bed, etc. Assume that there's nothing too serious about what you're hearing, by being cheerful but firm. Think of how many times you've had to encourage them to do things they've ended up really enjoying and you've felt glad you pushed them. Don't hand over authority by letting them have too much say in a situation that may be delicate for them for a while as they're adjusting. Tell them it's what you and Dad have arranged for them, that you want them to go, and that Dad is looking forward to seeing them. Remind them of some family news that they could try to remember to tell him about.

Before you take their resistance as meaning anything real or lasting about not liking their visits, consider that they may be expressing a number of different feelings and needs. In other words, get in touch with the context of their behaviour. More than anything your children need to feel you're enthusiastic about them going to their dad's place. They may just be wanting some reassurance about how much you really approve and what lengths you'll go to to support this important relationship.

Here are some ideas about context: they may feel they miss out on activities with you when they go away for the weekend; there doesn't seem to be enough time to do everything they're involved with where they are at the moment (at your place); they're sometimes bored at their dad's because there isn't enough to do (see below), and they're more used to you being around too; they may be feeling temporary anxieties about being away from you and their usual home; more of their favourite possessions and friends may be at your place; they may be uncomfortable about their dad's new lady friend and feel disloyal to you when they respond to her easily, or they prefer having their dad all to themselves rather than sharing him with a relative stranger (see Chapter 4); perhaps they're uncomfortable when their dad says things about you or asks them about you; they may be worried about whether you'll be OK without them, concerned you might be lonely, or they may be sensing their dad is sad and lonely and want to avoid having to deal with this; they probably dislike the handover from you to their dad, as it reminds them of the fact of you having separated and they sense tension between you; on the other hand, they may just want to watch a television show that they know you'll allow while their dad has different rules about viewing time!

As we've mentioned before, young children are very involved in the here and now and their reluctance may only mean they're engaged in something they want to continue. It's easy to mistake what is actually apprehension about the transition between one parent and the other for anxiety about or dislike for actually being with their dad.

All of the above are possible reasons behind their remarks. They are quite usual and understandable problems associated with getting used to having a to-and-fro life while their parents are also making their own adjustments to being separated. Try to keep communication open about their dad and don't let their apparent reluctance worry you. You probably will worry but try to remember that it's really very unlikely that a child would not want to spend time with one of their parents. Children want and need parental interest and attention, so you should try to think of their behaviour as not meaning they don't like being with him, but rather that some aspect of the shared arrangements is difficult for them at the moment. They shouldn't be given the idea that they can choose not to go, but should be reassured by your enthusiastic insistence. Any anxious response to their hesitance on your part may communicate to them that you aren't confident about them going, which isn't helpful.

If their reluctance to go persists, then it's time to arrange a talk with their dad. Make sure you listen to what he has to say, and avoid any suggestion that you suspect his way of caring for them has something to do with their behaviour. It'll be more effective to ask him for help and then ask him if he'd like to hear your ideas on the problem.

*'My daughter has said, "I don't want to stay the night with Dad"
when we've been discussing the fact that her dad is pushing for
overnight contact. I think this means she isn't ready for it, but her
father thinks I'm being overprotective and obstructive.'*

Many mothers, concerned to get things right for their children, would take this remark as meaning their child knows what they are and aren't ready for. In fact, *you* do, and what they're saying probably reflects many uncertainties, such as those we've discussed above.

Depending on the age of your child and whether she's stayed over with friends and family without her parents, there may be no reason why staying with her dad should be a problem for her, though it may be for you because of some anxieties you have to do with your feelings about him. If she's very young, spending the night away from you may require some adjustments by her, but her familiarity with her dad may mean she has more than one important attachment figure with whom she feels secure. If she's old enough to talk to you about it, she should be OK with it if she's seeing her dad regularly. So express your confidence in her and make your own judgment about what you think she's capable of managing. Put aside your anxieties that her routine will be disrupted, that she'll miss you or be distressed, and look forward to a night off! Remember you, like every parent, want your child to grow up, be independent and confident about new experiences. Listen to what reasons she seems to want to give you as to why she doesn't want to stay with her dad. Remarks about missing you when at Dad's don't usually mean a child can't manage without you; they may just want to reassure you that you weren't forgotten while they were having fun, and that they wish you'd been able to be there too. Your child has to get on with the reality of how things are now. You can say: 'It's nice you're thinking of me when you're away from me. I enjoy thinking of you having fun with Dad!'. Avoid saying you miss her too, because this may make her think you need her or are worrying about her. Try to make missing someone more like a happy reflection of secure and important bonds than something sad and negative. Talk about adventures away from each other and how nice it is when you're back together again. Normalise absences with Dad by likening them to times at school camps, social sleepovers, etc., and say, for example, 'It's nice now you're old enough to enjoy times doing your own thing, and I enjoy hearing about what you feel like telling me'.

If you decide to agree to your daughter having overnight stays, don't make the mistake of suggesting she ring you, or that you ring her. This might reassure *you*, but it may convey that you aren't sure she'll be all right, or that she might need you while she's away. This isn't helpful and may prevent her turning to her father to meet her needs when she's in his care, which will limit her sense of independence about being away from you. If her dad encourages her to ring you, well and good, but avoid suggesting to her that there's any doubt that she's OK or that her time with him can be renegotiated by contacting you. The time to do this is after she has had an overnight experience or two and you have listened to her and talked to her dad.

'Sam came home from his dad's the other day full of excitement as usual. He started to tell me something and then stopped himself in mid-sentence and said, "Oops, I'm not supposed to tell you anything, Dad said not to..."

'Usually I try not to ask him too much about what he's been up to so he doesn't feel I'm checking up on him and his father, but it upset me to think he'd been told not to talk to me when it seemed he wanted to, just as he chats away when he comes

home from kindy or a friend's place. What should I have said? Should I tell him it's OK to tell me things, or should I say, "It's all right, I don't need to know", or what?'

Sam may have got the idea (directly or indirectly) that he shouldn't or mustn't or isn't supposed to tell you anything about his time with Dad. But don't be tempted to fear the worst immediately by taking Sam's statement at face value, thinking that your child is specifically being told to keep secrets from you and that there are therefore sinister things you aren't meant to know. First, consider other reasons he could have made this statement which are less worrying.

He may be trying to make himself believe that, contrary to his hopes, his parents really are separated and therefore he must try to behave as if they are by establishing a boundary between their two households. He may be apprehensive about whether his father approves of how he's managing his new circumstances, so that 'Will Dad mind if I talk to Mum?' or 'Is that how I should behave if they're separated?' becomes 'Dad says not to say anything', which really means 'I'd better not in case he doesn't want me to'. In other words, Sam having sensed his dad wants to keep their time separate (perhaps he is further on with his new life, having been the one to leave the marriage) may have caused him to say he has been told not to tell you things. And, after all, he still needs parental authority and may want to enlist his dad to decide things for him rather than take responsibility for how to behave himself, which he probably doesn't know how to do. So it may just be his way of managing. Keep in mind that preschoolers and young children are fascinated by the idea of secrets. His remark may have nothing to do with separation-related adjustments; he and his dad may be preparing a surprise for you! Disenchantment about his dad on your part can make you forget innocent interpretations.

Welcome your child back from his time with his dad with enthusiasm. Say something like 'Had a great time, did you?' as a way of conveying that you genuinely hope he did. Then let him tell you what he wants you to know at his own pace. Tell him light-heartedly what you've been up to while he's been gone and he may think of telling you more. But don't make him go against what he's feeling is permitted by asking too many questions. Ask yourself whether you need to know more to show you're interested, or are you really checking up to see whether you approve of what they do together, such as how he was fed or what time he went to bed.

If his dad really is telling him to keep things secret you can't do anything about it anyway, and criticising his dad's apparent instructions to him will put Sam on the spot. You can remind him that he can tell you anything he wants to but that he doesn't have to. This will reassure him and release him from a sense of pressure about how to please both of you. You could add something, light-heartedly again, so that it doesn't sound critical, like 'I wouldn't have thought you had to keep secrets from me, but never mind, I'm not bothered, you just tell me what you feel it's OK to say'. Then you don't exactly say you agree with the practice of engaging children in conspiracies about you, but you accept it and don't blame Sam.

Finding the happy medium between being interested and being interfering is quite a skill. Young children often aren't very forthcoming about what's past and done, they're into the here and now, and sometimes seem unwilling to think back. It doesn't mean there's necessarily anything of concern that's being kept from you, although the situation may make you afraid there is. You've probably experienced welcoming your children home from school with a 'What did you do today?' question and found they say, 'Nothing much!', and you accept this as normal.

Keeping Mum and Dad's worlds separate is something children seem to do to avoid controversy or competition, or just because it seems easier that way. They need your interest, but they also need to feel free to sort out how they manage their two worlds, without having to worry too much about how to please everybody or what kind of comments you might make.

'I really don't think John (my ex) should have the children for the weekend and then leave them with his parents for most of the time. They tell me he goes out in the evening and that they often have people around. Surely he should be spending one-to-one time with them? I'm worried that they're getting the message he hasn't got time for them. I'm thinking of trying to insist that he exclude his parents because the children's time is supposed to be with him, not a whole crowd of other people.'

It's common for parents to feel concerned about how their former partner is using their time with their children. You may be disappointed in what you're hearing from them, but you have to keep in mind that if he can't see how valuable spending one-to-one time with them is, then there's very little you can do about it, and your disapproval certainly won't help them. We've talked elsewhere about the need for parents to let go. If your ex-partner is using the comfort, support and convenience of his parents to help him with his parenting responsibilities, then that's how he is. And it's not all bad. They are your children's grandparents, after all. They may be very concerned, as paternal grandparents often are, that your separation is going to result in them losing contact with these grandchildren, so they're only too ready to offer their hospitality and assistance. Your children's links with their father's family are important to them and their relationship may be mutually reinforcing. Do you disapprove of them seeing their grandparents as such or is it just that you think the children need more attention from their father? Many people reassociate closely with their parents after a separation because it's an important source of security, now that marriage has disappointed them. Also, your ex-partner may be uncertain about how to use his time imaginatively without his parents' help.

You can't very well tell their father to adopt your values and standards about parenting. He'll feel controlled and criticised. Try not to show your disapproval to the children, or inquire too closely about who they spend their time with. After their next weekend away, use the listening skills you're now becoming familiar with and decide whether what they have to say suggests that they do mind all these other people being around and they want more time with their dad. Help them to label their feelings and to think of what they might do about it, such as asking their dad if they can go out together more, for instance. However, remember that your children's accounts of how much their dad goes out during their weekends together or how often he is with them at his parents' home may be a bit inaccurate! Don't forget that you can always ask to meet with their dad to review how the arrangements are going and suggest tactfully that the children may be wanting more attention from him.

'My son, who's nine years old, has started to say during our time together, usually towards the end of a visit, that he wants to come and live with me. This worries me and I think maybe I should do something about what he seems to be feeling.'

This is a difficult statement to field if it catches you unawares because you probably feel pleased that he says this. It makes you feel loved and valued and that your efforts to be a part-time parent are worth it. You should welcome his words at the time as a statement of how much he loves you and enjoys his time with you.

Maybe you've always wanted to be his main caretaker but his mum wouldn't consider this and so you couldn't do much about it. Depending on how you feel about his mum, you may be afraid he's saying something significant about what living with his mum is like. Despite these feelings you should respond by saying something like 'We sure do have a good time together, don't we?'; and/or 'Next time you come isn't so long away, and we'll plan some more good things to do'; and/or 'Yes, it's sad you have to go, but Mum will be looking forward to seeing you, and so will I for next time [etc.]'. You could say, 'It would be nice to be together all the time', but you should add, 'It can't happen because Mum and I separated, but we still have a good time, don't we?'. A hug and an 'I love you heaps' would be reassuring, if this is in your style range. So be positive about him leaving you, acknowledging that partings can be sad. This will tell him you're in charge and OK, that his going is OK with you (even if it isn't), and it demonstrates good handling of feelings.

Before you decide whether you should do anything more about what he's saying, consider the possible meanings behind it: to recap, he's probably telling you in his own way how much he loves you, which is, of course, wonderful and reinforcing and should be reciprocated as such. He may want you to reassure him of how much you love him. He may wish to communicate his ongoing wish that his parents were still together; how difficult he finds the forthcoming handover because it's such an immediate reminder of his parents' separateness; what fun he has with you (which doesn't necessarily mean he doesn't have fun with his mum too); or that he sometimes worries about how you manage without him.

If your time together involves lots of leisure activities at weekends and during school holidays he'll obviously not want this to end — he might think that living with you all the time would mean this much fun always! His time with his mum may well be associated with weekday routines, homework and other commitments and not so much one-to-one attention, especially if she has a new partner and you don't.

You could talk with his mum about your relationship with your son and discuss possible variations to the arrangements together so that he spends more time with you, if you think this is what you both want. If you suggest he tells his mum what he's said to you, then there's a danger that you'll create a conflict of loyalty for him. He probably won't be able to tell her he wants to live with you, even if he really thinks this, and you'll be reinforcing the idea that he can rearrange things, or that you really do want him to live mainly with you rather than his mum.

However much you'd like him to be with you more, you should not let a nine-year-old think he can choose between his parents and alter the arrangements. Consider that he can't possibly know what it would feel like to be without his mum or to live with feeling he'd chosen you in preference to her.

Leave it for a while, keep listening to him, and then ask his mum for a meeting to review his care and offer more time with him, if you really think this is what he needs.

'My seven-year-old has lately been using some bad language at home, and refusing to cooperate with things like cleaning his teeth and finishing his food. Yesterday he said to me that his dad doesn't make him do things like I do. I really resent having to have confrontations about these basic and important things that obviously his father isn't supporting me on.'

Getting used to having less control over your child's development because he spends time regularly away from you with another influential person is a major adjustment you're going to have to make, especially if you've been very closely involved in your child's care. Dad may never have spent much time on his own with him before, while you have usually been there, making sure, as mothers do, that all these things get done. Parenting practices (along with finances) are a major source of marital distress, so you may well be worried about how the children will fare in your estranged partner's care now that you aren't there as a moderator any more, because you know you have fundamental differences about what is important. If your son is to continue a relationship with his dad you have to do a bit of letting go. So does his dad, as he may disagree with some aspects of your parenting style too.

Don't be afraid to assert the standards you have for your child when he is in your care. Without explicitly criticising his dad, remind him firmly what the rules about bad language and personal hygiene are in your household. Dad may be choosing to let these things go because he doesn't want their limited time together to be full of confrontations. (This is, in fact, misguided of him, and we shall be discussing the importance of parental authority in Chapter 5.) Remember that it is a normal part of growing up to begin to assert your independence from your parents and to test them out. Oppositional behaviour is quite commonly beginning to be expressed towards their mothers by boys the age of your son, as part of the process of individuation. That is, they have a developmental need to become separate from your femaleness and begin to take on a sense of their own maleness. He may also be challenging you as a way of expressing his anger about your separation.

Whatever the explanation, and it's probably a mixture of reasons, your firm insistence that he must oblige is required. Explain that Dad has his way of doing things because he is different to you, to counteract your son's comment that his dad is less strict than you are about these important things concerning his care. You are trying to raise your son to be independent and responsible, so tell him you think he should clean his teeth, that he should think about the consequences for others of using bad language, wherever he is, and that growing up involves becoming independent in more and more of his self-care.

'When the kids come back from spending the weekend with their dad, they seem unruly, unsettled and uncooperative. It takes me ages to settle them down. With school the next day this isn't good for them and their teacher says she can tell when they've had a weekend with him. I think their father lets them stay up late and provides too many excitements for them. I really am thinking I should change the arrangements.'

It's very hard for a parent to have to manage children whose mood and behaviour appears to be very much the result of their ex-partner's style of parenting. You feel as if you're dealing with the hard bits you aren't responsible for on a Sunday night when everyone should be winding down peacefully for another week. Keep in mind that some of their exuberance is natural after being away from you and settling back into your care. Try to see it as positive that they've had a good time, and keep in mind that they're probably tired. Be calmly firm about rudeness being unacceptable and allow them some winding-down time, which they'll probably respond to by resuming normal activities like having a meal or watching a favourite television show. Don't expect them to tell you much about what they've been doing, and avoid inquiring about whether they had late nights because it will probably come across as if you're checking up on them. For the first few months they are getting used to this new routine for being with both their parents and they will settle down to it better if you are enthusiastic about their return. Try not to let their mood irritate you as this may convey to them that their time with their dad is a hassle to you. You probably feel it is sometimes, but they shouldn't be made to think this too often.

Given time they will probably become less excitable, and perhaps their dad will slow down on the exciting treats as he becomes more confident about his time with them. Meanwhile, it may help you to get ready for them to arrive home exuberant by bracing yourself mentally for the onslaught of high spirits. Before you open a discussion with their dad about changing the arrangements, consider whether doing this would really address the problem you have. If you're thinking of asking them to be returned earlier in the day, this may make Sunday nights less hectic but they may well still arrive a bit wound up.

'My ex-husband has continued to be interfering and critical of me, often in front of the children when he collects them or drops them back. He's always wanted to have them mainly in his care and he's still angry that the court didn't rule in his favour several years ago. My nine-year-old son Christopher says things like "Daddy hates you!" and he gets very angry with me at times. I always try to calm him down and tell him Daddy doesn't really mean it, but it really wears me down trying to be positive all the time. Is there anything I can do to get across to his father how bad for the children his behaviour is? Will it affect Christopher permanently?'

It sounds as though your children have been having a very difficult time. I expect you often wonder whether it would be better if they didn't see him at all rather than having to go through this. There's no doubt that this kind of ongoing conflict is bad for children, but it is difficult to exclude a father who wants to be with them. If you have ruled out the possibility of reducing the frequency of their contact with him, which probably means going back to court, then your only option is to look at what *you* can do differently. You should identify and accept Christopher's anger and say you under-stand why he's feeling it; say that it must be very hard for him to think that his father hates his mother, when he wants to love them both.

His father shouldn't be saying these things but you can't stop him. Have an honest look at whether some of your behaviour at changeover times creates opportunities for insults which you could avoid by making changes yourself. For example, if you're keen to give the children a welcome and see how they are, do you present yourself at the front door trying to engage civilly with their father in the hope that he will converse helpfully with you? If this doesn't work because he can't be civil, perhaps you could minimise the opportunities you give him for making these sorts of comments. Could the children say goodbye to their father, let themselves in and come and find you? You could tell them to do this if you think they're old enough. Have you tried arranging for them to be picked up and dropped off somewhere you don't have to be present, such as a friend's or relation's place or their school?

Remind Christopher that his dad's anger is aimed at you, and help him not to feel responsible for it or that he must imitate it to please his father. Try to make your conversations into general ones about difficult emotions and about how people who behave badly aren't all bad. Sadly, he has to accept that his father cannot behave responsibly towards people and he will be influenced by this. He may well grow up affected by the dysfunctional relationship between his parents and it will most likely affect his adult partnerships somehow. However, he probably has other male role models in his life and this will also influence him, as will your dignified refusal to enter into arguments with his father.

I would try to communicate with Christopher's father calmly but assertively, at the time these difficult exchanges occur, that you dislike his behaviour and that it's no way to treat a fellow human. Do this in front of the children so they know you don't accept it, and then withdraw indoors (or wherever). I wouldn't say, 'Daddy doesn't really mean it', because Christopher knows he probably does. I would say: 'Daddy was really angry with me again today, wasn't he? I don't like that, and it's not nice for you, is it?'. Then move on. You're not glossing over the reality of what goes on, and you're showing honestly where the responsibility lies without drawing Christopher into it. We'll be looking further into managing emotional expressions in Chapter 7.

'What should I say to my two children when we've arranged for their mum to come and pick them up, I've got them all ready and excited, and she doesn't turn up on time and sometimes not at all? I get a telephone call later just when we've all started getting on with something else. Their disappointment is difficult to deal with.'

Creating an expectation in your children that you will be there for them and then letting them down can be devastating for them, but it happens. As with Christopher, above, children have to confront their parents' failings, sometimes sooner rather than later in life. Sadly, younger children especially tend to blame themselves for not being valuable or loveable enough to the parent letting them down. But you have a lot of power to give them a sense of their value to *you*, which will compensate for this. If your separation was quite recent, their mother may be going through a bad patch emotionally and may become more reliable as she gets used to shared parenting. Perhaps timekeeping was an issue in your marriage, and your differences are now highlighted.

As we saw earlier, shared parenting often requires you to guide your children through feelings and manage behaviour that you didn't contribute to. Acknowledge to yourself that anyone who upsets your children will get to you and you'll be likely to feel a surge of protective rage. But this is *your* anger, so deal with it without involving the children; if you transmit your exasperation to them it won't help. This is another situation where you must keep the full intensity of your feelings to yourself, but you can acknowledge that you feel disappointed. There's nothing wrong with saying that you're a bit cross with Mum for being late but say it in a light-hearted way, as if that's your problem not theirs, which, of course, it is. This is authentic communication, consistent with the event, and shows that loved ones make you cross sometimes, which is just life.

Once they've noticed Mum hasn't arrived, comment to them that she's late again, that she's trying to get here (which she probably is) and that it's good they are all ready for her when she does arrive. If they seem quite upset, explain that sometimes people don't think that being on time is important and they don't think of it causing disappointment; that it's always upsetting when you're looking forward to something and you have to wait. Reassure them that Mum loves them, even if it doesn't seem that way when she doesn't get there on time. You'll be confidently showing them how to cope when loved ones do disappointing things.

'I was a bit stuck the other day when my son (eight years old) said to me he'd had a boring time at his dad's. I asked what they'd been up to and he said Dad made him watch the football with him and then he spent time in the office and on the phone. I've always thought his father ought to give him more attention. I don't know what to say to this, and I can hardly tell his father how to look after him.'

First of all, think of all the possible meanings behind your son's comment before you take it too seriously, or decide you need to do anything about it. Identify with his position, and check any assumptions you might bring to your interpretation of it. Perhaps your son *is* bored sometimes. Is this necessarily a bad thing? Ask him how he deals with boredom and listen to him acceptingly. He may have had a fairly full weekend but was bored for a while and remembered this because it was less pleasant than the fun times, or maybe he felt uneasy when they weren't actually doing anything and his dad needed to get a few things done. Maybe they're both feeling a little awkward, not having spent much time on their own together without Mum. Perhaps spending time with each of you separately highlights your different approaches to parenting and he's noticing this. Maybe his dad does believe in leaving him to his own devices more than you do, and now he cannot refer to you and receive your attention when he feels he cannot engage his father, because you aren't there. He is having to get used to this new way of being with his father.

Find out what he would like to do at his dad's and encourage him to ask for what he wants from his father. You're helping him to generate his own solution, and not assuming his 'difficulties' belong to you. Maybe he's better able to amuse himself with you because all his things are there, and not at his dad's place. You could suggest he takes something with him when he goes next time.

Keep in mind that he may have a need to play down his enjoyment of time with his dad and bring home negative comments about it because he thinks it's what you want to hear. He may be uncertain, because of how he thinks you feel about his dad, of whether you approve of his visits. Therefore, he may not feel comfortable saying to you that he had a good time there. Perhaps his father could make more effort to do things with him, but your son has to negotiate his relationship with his father in his own way, and you can't be much of an influence, as you say, on how they spend their time together. Store his remark away somewhere in your mind and don't be too concerned about it.

Key Points for Shared Parenting

- Sharing your child, especially when they are young, with other caretakers is difficult because you feel very responsible for their wellbeing, as indeed you should. This is especially true when you're parenting on your own. In the months immediately after separating many parents feel their confidence in how to parent effectively is undermined. You can't control or even know much about your child's experiences away from you, although you may very much want to: see above. They need to feel you trust their other parent so they can be free to enjoy this important relationship.

- Try to be confident about how you parent and stick to your usual way of doing things, even though you may know that your ex-partner does things very differently, and does some things you definitely disapprove of. Your children will not be confused, provided both of you make your expectations of your children when they're with you clear, so they know where they stand.

- Listen to your children and field their remarks attentively but without reading too much into them. If you take their often random remarks too literally you may give yourself unnecessary worry. Remind yourself that your child needs your support, not your anxiety. Even if you do decide their remark is worrying, ask yourself whether you can do much anyway, other than acknowledge that getting used to being separated is difficult for people some of the time.

- When your child says critical, negative or resentful things to you about their other parent that, quite frankly, you agree with, try to respond in general terms about human differences in the way people do things. Invent a few excuses (even though you probably don't think your ex-partner deserves any!). This way you're not siding with your child against their other parent by agreeing with them; you're accepting the remark without actually disagreeing with it, because you don't. This will make your child feel listened to, and will make them feel free to find their own way to negotiate a relationship which you are no longer part of, which is healthy and useful. It will convey some respect for individual differences, which they need to feel you have, so that they know it's OK to say things. They'll respect you and be reassured by you showing you won't be drawn into a competition between you and your ex-partner.

- Don't lose sight of what lies within quite normal limits and is just part of growing up. It's easy to worry when you're parenting on your own, and it's common to be oversensitive to your children's remarks because you feel guilty about what your separation is doing to them or because you're angry about your ex-partner. Consult a child development professional or a good parenting manual (see suggested readings) to reassure yourself about your child's behaviour.

CHAPTER 4

NEW ADULTS

Sooner or later you'll probably want to bring a new adult into your life and therefore into your children's lives. Both you and your ex-partner are likely to find a new partner in time. Perhaps there's been someone associated with the breakdown of your relationship, which always complicates things emotionally. One of you feels rejected and replaced, anxious that your children will form attachments to this rival that you're probably uncomfortable about; the other wants to get on with having the children get to know this person and be part of a stepfamily. Maybe you've had a reasonably amicable separation and talked about the likelihood of new partners. However, it's very likely that when the time comes you won't feel quite as 'together' about it as you thought you would, even if you both have new friends. This is because you'll be thinking about how it'll affect the children and whether the new person will respect your role as their parent. Some people have anxieties about their former partner having someone else even if they themselves have, anxieties which can contribute to unhelpful attitudes about their children's freedom to accept this new person. These feelings are understandable in the circumstances, but they need to be faced squarely and taken into account rather than denied or 'swept under the carpet'.

Separation requires children to make some important adjustments, as we've seen. Having a new adult in their lives, one who takes the place of a loved parent at their other parent's side, is a challenge they don't need in addition to getting used to their parents being separated. It should be obvious that this will present problems, but it's surprising how many parents, inspired by a new relationship, forget their children's position and are impatient with their former partner's difficulty in accepting that they have someone new. It's as if, after a reasonable interval, they expect their former partner to feel it's OK to be with someone else simply because they themselves do. It often isn't like this! If you can postpone introducing a new partner to the children it's easier for them, especially if your 'ex' is feeling bitter and upset about being replaced and anxious about the children's reaction to your new partner. For example, your former wife may want to be accepting and declare that she's OK about it, but when the time comes she may find it difficult not to project her own feelings onto the children, unwittingly assuming they'll have difficulties with your new partner, because she herself does. Keeping your new love-life separate from your parenting responsibilities for a time so as to allow everyone to get used to the break-up will help everyone with the adjustments of separating, even though doing this may not suit your own need to get on with your new life.

Problems in stepfamilies are at least *as* common as they are in traditional families, if not more so, because people don't prepare for them properly and have idealistic expectations that the strength of the new relationship itself will ensure everything works out. This is seldom true, as many stepfamilies find out later (you'll see this in Chapter 5). It's always easier to have at least a year elapse during which the children can feel reassured that their relationship with both their parents is going to be honoured attentively and committedly by both of them, before introducing new partners. It should be even longer if there are unresolved financial and parenting issues being disputed in court.

However, we have to 'get real' and acknowledge that many parents don't time their 'relationship lives' all that wisely because they have personal needs that they put first and don't think they should have to consider the consequences for others. Having said this, some separations which are sensitively managed and amicable are not so difficult for children to adjust to, and they can take to a parent's new partner with apparent ease because they feel their other parent is OK about it. Children usually accept new people readily, especially someone they know is making you happy. If one of you has someone new, it's sometimes a relief for children when the other does; it sort of evens things out for everyone. But some reticence, and even resentment, is not unusual, however helpful their other parent is being about you having someone new, because this person represents the permanent nature of their parents' separation and the impossibility of there ever being the reconciliation they may have been hoping for. So keep in mind that children have their own feelings about a new person, which do not necessarily directly originate from attitudes on the part of their other parent.

All this advising caution is not to say that a new relationship which satisfies you and makes you happy isn't a good thing for your wellbeing, and hence your parenting energy and enthusiasm. It just means you shouldn't be blind to the effect it's going to have on the children from your past, and perhaps their other parent. Sensible planning, including generous lead times, is a very worthwhile investment in your children's emotional future.

'My kids say they don't want contact with their mum's new boyfriend, but she seems to be planning that he'll be around when they're with her. What do I say, when I don't approve of him being with them? I think she should be spending time with them on her own, not involving him with our children so soon.'

If your children are to spend time with their mum, she has to be in charge of decisions she makes about who she shares that time with. You may not approve (and it probably is unwise of her, at least to begin with) of her planning for her friend to be around when the children are visiting, but there isn't much you can do about it. Once again, look at what your children say in context. It may not be that they have formed any kind of opinion of their mum's new boyfriend's character, whatever you might think of him. They may be saying they don't want him there because they see him as the cause of the break-up they would rather hadn't happened. They may sense you are sad about the split and hence about his part in it. That's hard to hide from them and would make it difficult for them to be easygoing about his presence.

In other words, get in touch with possible meanings behind their comment, then try to say something genuine but not inhibiting, like: 'Mum's chosen her friend and maybe you'd rather not share her with him. That's understandable, but off you go and it'll probably be OK for you. I'll be fine, I'm going to do some jobs around here, maybe the mowing'. This is light-hearted, reassuring and conveys your confidence that they will manage, knowing it's OK with you. Even though you disapprove, you haven't said so, which would criticise their mum. If you know they know you disapprove, you'd better say so outright and make it clear to them that is your feeling about him, but that you nevertheless really want them to have a go at accepting him because Mum obviously wants them to.

Say something that makes it clear your feelings are separate from theirs, like 'Yes, I do feel a bit hesitant about Chris getting to know you just yet, but those are my feelings and I don't want you to be concerned about them, so off you go [etc.]'. If their comments persist you should still try to be understanding and encouraging. Mention them to their mum if you think she'll be prepared to listen to your observations about the children.

'The children came home last weekend saying, "Dad's got a new girlfriend and we don't like her!". I didn't know what to say to this!'

Again, try quickly to key in to what they're really saying. It may be a test of how you'll react, or an expression of how they'd prefer he was still with you, or maybe she took too much of their father's attention, or she tried too hard to endear herself to them so they felt the relationship was forced upon them. Perhaps she was uneasy about how to be with them and so they felt uncomfortable about her, sensing her apprehension. They may be expressing their resentment about anybody 'usurping' your rightful position at their father's side. This is the stuff of wicked stepmother mythology! Some initial resentment is normal under the circumstances. They may just be temporarily uncomfortable about her. If you show too much concern they may not feel they can mention things about time spent with their dad. Also, they may just be saying they don't like her because they think you want them to disapprove of her. Don't buy into this or you may encourage them to come home and say negative and critical things because doing this attracts your interest.

Whatever your feelings about her, don't forget you want your children to be able to get on with other people. Your feelings about their dad's girlfriend are separate from theirs.

Try not to be too anxious about how to respond. Ask them why they think they don't like her so as to pay attention to their comment and invite them to say more. You may get a comfortingly childish response about her awful earrings or something! Then move on to some other topic, but keep a 'watchful' ear for further comments about her and try to help them accept this person as best you can, just as you would try to make suggestions to help them adjust to any other person they had to get along with. At least they're telling you something about time with their dad.

'What's best for children when it comes to new partners? Is it OK to have friends I'm dating call around? How do I explain questions about new partners when I don't even know whether a friendship will lead to anything longer term? I'm worried about what they might say to their dad about new people they've met.'

Your value system about what you want to transmit to your children will guide you in this. Depending on how recent your separation was there may be issues for them about how soon you might be seen to be replacing their father and meeting your own quite natural needs to explore new relationships and leave the past behind. You may find that it's easier all round if you concentrate on your relationship life as a single adult at times when the children are with their father. It's not that you're keeping it a secret; rather you are avoiding complications for the children and having to worry about your own divided loyalties. This may mean you're more relaxed about it and that's better for you. If new friends are keen to endear themselves to your children and they respond enthusiastically, your children may feel disillusioned when they fade out of your life. Nevertheless, children generally take new people in their stride and they should know you have partnership needs as well as parenting responsibilities. If their father is coping OK with your separation he may not be concerned about what they may tell him about new people they meet. If he isn't then it may be worthwhile you keeping them out of the forefront of family life for a while. Depending on the ages of your children, new friends sleeping over may be an issue for them. Sharing your bed may well mean something more permanent to them than they are ready for, such as marriage and long-term commitment, whatever the relationship may mean for you.

When you've considered all this, you'll be able to work out what suits you, your children's position and the possible reactions of their dad. Introduce callers as acquaintances and answer their questions about their status in your life with an 'I don't know at this stage, but we'll see'. Also, make sure you don't get too exclusively involved too soon so they feel they've lost you to him rather suddenly when they need you to be available to them just as you always have been.

'Robbie suddenly started calling Joe (my new partner) by his name when he'd been calling him 'Dad'. I rather like the children calling him Dad because it seems to mean they accept him. Has he been told not to by his father? Should I say anything?'

No, you shouldn't. Robbie may have been told not to call his stepfather 'Dad', which is a pity, but you can't do anything about it. His dad may not have said anything to him, and Robbie was just trying to sort everything out in his mind.

Robbie won't ever forget who his father and stepfather are and their different places in his life. The only way this could happen would be if Robbie was very young when you separated and wasn't seeing his father and you were pretending Joe was his real dad. The best favour you can do for Robbie is to show him you don't mind at all and that he can use whatever name comes out at the time. If he asks you what he should call Joe, say: 'Whatever suits you, I'm not fussed. He probably does feel like a dad sometimes so "Dad" or "Joe" is OK with me'. Don't bother to ask about what his dad might have said about names, even though you might want to know. Let him be free to respond to his dad in his own way without your interference in matters you have views about. If he does say, 'Dad doesn't like me calling Joe "Dad"', ask him how that makes him feel, show you understand, but don't pass judgment. Tell him again you don't mind if he wants to refer to Joe as 'Joe' in your family and suggest that might make it easier to get things right with Dad. You could add that Dad maybe feels a bit on the outer now that Joe's around and he likes the reassurance that he's still just as much 'Dad' as he ever was. You're offering an interpretation of his dad's position which may help Robbie not to worry about it, without imposing it on him.

Names quite often become a problem for parents and therefore for their children. This is always because a parent has some personal insecurity about their relationship with their child, or some anger about the insult of an apparent takeover by a new adult in their child's life. This can be very difficult for a child, and it is an unnecessary extra stress when they're struggling to get pleasing their parents right!

'Lately my daughter's been coming home grumpy and withdrawn from her weekends with her dad. I know he's got a new girlfriend and I'm worried that she might be upset by this. She's fourteen years old.' ·

Think of all the possible reasons for what you've observed other than the existence of her dad's girlfriend, reminding yourself of other times when your daughter may have been withdrawn and grumpy. Ask yourself what *you* feel about her dad having a girlfriend and be honest with yourself about the answer. Your daughter may not mind about it just because you do!

Tell your daughter next time she arrives back from being with her father that you've noticed this change in her and ask her if anything in particular is bothering her. She may not want to say what it is, or even admit she's been quiet, because she doesn't know herself or she doesn't want to upset you. She may be expressing discomfort about the changeover between the two households she's now part of. If part of the reason *is* the girlfriend, she may be concerned about how you feel and mightn't want to say anything. She might be ashamed of her withdrawal and not want to acknowledge it. She might be tired and aware that when she returns to you she has to face homework and other things that weekends away prevent her getting done. Her dad's girlfriend might be really nice and she's feeling guilty about liking her. Many other interpretations are possible, and we've discussed how moving between two parents is often difficult and sad for children, and how making room for new partners takes some adjusting.

Listen to what she has to say, identify with her position sympathetically, and acknowledge that adjusting to new situations is hard. Don't take what she says too literally and worry about it. She will manage her feelings in her own way if you support her without telling her what her feelings are, or should be. If she says she's uncomfortable about the girlfriend, invite her to say more, help her identify and name her feelings, show you understand even if you don't agree, and remind her how family life can cause all sorts of uncomfortable, confusing feelings. Take the content of her comments with a grain of salt, despite the fact that you may be fascinated by girlfriend information, and just be there patiently for her.

'How do I introduce my new friend? I'm concerned about timing because I know it will upset my ex-wife. Sue is really keen to meet the children and she's starting to feel that because I haven't introduced them to her, it means I'm not committed to our relationship.'

First, you have to decide whether *you* want to keep your time with the children separate from your new friendship. Is there really any hurry for Sue to meet them? Can you reassure her in other ways about your relationship? She's probably impatient partly because she knows they are an important part of your life, and partly because she wants to feel you're committed to her. Perhaps you'd better ask yourself whether you think it's a big step for the relationship to involve your children in it, and if you do, then you can understand why Sue is keen to become involved with them. But think carefully about how this is all going to seem from your children's and their mother's point of view, and put them first. Your ex-wife probably needs more time to accept this new development.

If you do want to involve Sue soon, you should tell the children's mother in advance that you're going to do this. It may be harder for her if she hears about Sue from the children. Introduce Sue at a fun meeting place to start with so she doesn't seem immediately to be a definite fixture in residence with you. Say something to the children along the lines of 'I'd like you to meet Sue next weekend, she's my new friend and she's coming to the zoo with us'.

When the time comes, just be very low-key about her so they can accept her in their own way without too many expectations arising from your anxieties. She should try to be an interesting 'extra' to start with, so discuss this with her in advance so she can raise any apprehensions she has with you then. Let things progress gradually from there, taking care that you still have plenty of one-to-one time with the children. If they ask 'Is Sue your girlfriend?' and you're concerned about their mum's reaction, you could say: 'Yes, we're going out and we'll see how it works out in time; Mum knows about her [they may know this] and I think it might be hard for her to think of me with someone else, and I can understand that may make it awkward for you'. That way you've said clearly how it is for you, you've shown you know how it is for them, but you haven't told them how they should feel or made them think Sue shouldn't be mentioned. This will help them deal with their mum's reactions (which may not be as bad as you fear), if you've faced it squarely with the children, rather than kept things secret or left unsaid, and therefore left to their imagination.

'I told the children's mother I wanted to start slowly involving my girlfriend with the children when they're with me. She was a bit upset and started talking about all sorts of things that happened when we were together. The next weekend she rang and said the children didn't want to come if SHE was going to be there. I really feel this is emotional blackmail. But I said I wouldn't do it, so as not to miss out on seeing the children. What should I say to them, or should I just leave it?'

Your feeling blackmailed is understandable. Many fathers report feeling that they are the victims of their ex-wives' power over their relationships with their children, and this can be very diminishing. Losing your sense of freedom can make you angry and resentful, so that you stand on principle about what you want to do, which isn't always helpful. You probably re-acted as if the children's mother must either be enlisting the children in her anxieties about you having a girlfriend or has spoken for them. She may have transmitted her anxieties to them so they felt they had to say this or express hesitancy about coming, which she has interpreted as them also resenting you having someone new.

If it isn't all that important that you do involve your girlfriend yet, then consider leaving it for a while. Even though this is 'giving in' to your ex-wife, your relationship with your children is at stake, and maybe it will be worth hanging on for a bit longer to consolidate your relationship with them further and to give their mum more time.

You should say something to the children next time they see you, on the basis that their mum may have involved them in the issue. It'll do no harm if she hasn't, because you'll be preparing them for later on. Say something like: 'I spoke to Mum about my friend and that I wanted you to meet her. She seemed a bit uncertain about how you'd feel about this, so I'll leave it for a while, I think. Her name is Julie and we're seeing each other regularly. I'd like you to meet her one of these days, and I hope you'll like her'. You're being low-key, sowing the seeds of a future introduction, and showing you understand the position it may put the children in with their mum, without making too much of this.

Leave it for a while and then bring it up again with their mum and see if she's softened her attitude at all. If she doesn't respond and you feel she's been unreasonable about this issue for too long, you may want to push things along without her 'permission'. Assert yourself by introducing Julie anyway, but you should tell your ex-wife yourself that it's happened, before or as you return the children. See what happens; it may all blow over with more time. The children will survive, especially if you show patient understanding of their situation.

Key Points for Successful Beginnings with New Partners

- Don't rush your children into accepting new partners; give them time.

- Be prepared to face the reality that some people find it very difficult to accept their ex-partner having someone new, and sustain unhelpful resentment about it for some time. However much you might regard this as unreasonable, there isn't much you can do to change it.

- Make sure new friends don't steal the limelight too much during your time with the children by taking a lot of your attention, especially to start with. It may well be good for the long-term prospects of the relationship if your new partner can be independently engaged with their own life while you concentrate on your children.

- Sort out with the new person what sort of relationship they are going to have with your children; don't leave it just to take care of itself. Agree that they take the role of an interesting, low-key 'extra'. Discourage any girlfriend you may have from doing too many motherly things with the children to start with, even if they naturally tend to go to her for such things.

- Don't be too concerned about names. First names may well be easier all round, but avoid correcting your children; let them use whatever name comes naturally.

- Avoid letting your children get too close to a series of new partners. The end of each friendship is a loss to the children if they've got on well with them. Involve new partners about whom you're reasonably serious, taking into account the likely attitude of your children's other parent.

- To begin with accept some reservations by your children about new partners as emanating from *them* rather than from unhelpful attitudes on the part of their other parent. Even if every adult is being accepting and helpful, sorting out new partners can take children time. Be patient and understanding of their position when you know their other parent is communicating resentment about a new partner to them — the other parent is in a very difficult position, so acknowledge this when the opportunity to do so arises in conversation.

CHAPTER 5

NEW FAMILIES

Once you've decided to make a new relationship more than just a dating one, and you start living together and/or marry, you've entered the challenging new realm of stepfamily life. As we've suggested earlier, this is not without its hazards, despite your optimism and confidence about your new partnership. The most important predictor of achieving a functional stepfamily is your willingness to prepare for it using foresight and good timing and to nurture it regularly as you go along. As the new couple at the head of the stepfamily, your ability to plan together and anticipate the many challenges that await you is the key ingredient in your success. This is now being more generally recognised, and there are a number of helpful books available; and, as usual, we'll give you some suggested guidelines at the end of this chapter.

New adult partnerships often involve new children too, either living with you all the time or visiting for contact with a parent. It can all be quite complicated. For instance, if Dad has a new partner, the partner may have children whom she cares for most of the time, and so Dad living with them, with his own children joining in some of the time, is the pattern. Depending on the timing it may be uncomfortable for one parent to be seeing someone else's children more than they see their own. The children have to get on as a 'sort of family' when they're all together, and they may not necessarily take to each other just because the two parents have teamed up, though there's every chance they will. The other common scenario is when Mum teams up with a man who is a father whose children see him regularly. They are not always part of their stepmum's home and must somehow fit in comfortably when they are.

In either of the above situations a new baby may arrive who is the child of a newer partnership and doesn't go away regularly to be with an important person outside of the immediate family. Half-brothers and half-sisters are bound by blood and there is often more time for adjustments to be made before these kinds of bonds are really starting to be established. There's time for children to get used to the idea of Mum or Dad having a baby with someone else. 'Stepsiblings' have no common history, and quite often it's a relationship with a fairly sudden start soon after a separation, though both 'sets' of children may be accustomed to being part of more than one family. However, they may see more of each other and develop stronger bonds than if they were related biologically. So it's often more than just getting on together with someone else's children, or the 'invasion' of yours on a regular basis: it's two sets of children having to get on together some or all of the time, and later, maybe, the family expands even further with the addition of someone whose relations are different again! No wonder there are hazards, and yet it seems everybody's doing it these days with great hopes.

'My ex-husband has recently moved in with his new partner and her two children. To begin with, our son seemed quite excited about having playmates laid on for him when he visited his dad.

But lately he doesn't seem so keen to go over there. Could there be a problem? Can I help him?'

Your son was probably full of optimism at the novelty of the new situation, but now that the initial excitement has worn off a bit, he's found he has some adjusting to do. He's now faced with the fact that when he goes there, family events have taken place which he wasn't part of so he feels a bit 'on the outer'. He's realised his dad spends a lot more time with someone else's children than he does with his own son. These other children have their own territory established in this home, and his may be set up just for his visits because of space limitations. He is an only child and hasn't experienced being in a family with other children who have a lifelong sibling bond of their own which he doesn't share. This may make him particularly sensitive to receiving less of his father's attention than he'd like to have, or he's been used to having. If you're on your own, staying with you where he's got you all to himself may seem an attractive alternative, especially, perhaps, when things don't quite go his way. Hopefully, his father is aware of this and is doing what he can to help him fit in, making some separate time for him during his stays.

When your boy is due to go there and is showing the hesitancy you've noticed, use the encouragement we discussed in Chapter 3. Ask him how he feels about the other children and acceptingly listen to what he has to say. Approach your conversation from the standpoint of helping him fit in with a new group just as he has had to mix in other new group settings. This will help you not to sound too concerned or alarmist, and will show your confidence in him. Don't be too disconcerted if he isn't very forthcoming. He may not be able to put his feelings into words, or even want to talk about it.

Don't forget the possibility that his hesitancy may not be to do with these other children, and consider the alternative explanations we've discussed elsewhere, particularly in Chapter 3. Give him time and he will probably adjust all right. If you feel able to approach his dad yourself, tell him about what you've noticed.

'I've formed a relationship with a mother at my children's school, and I'm living with her and her three children now. Sometimes before and after school we all cross paths and everyone seems rather awkward. My children look self-conscious and even seem to avoid Suzie's kids, though I know they've been good friends. It seems tragic and I don't want my children behaving rudely. Should I say anything to them?'

You have created a situation which is difficult for your children, and probably for Suzie's too, with good reason. You seem to be expecting them to be OK about something which is obviously not at all easy for them. They don't know how to behave towards you when they see you with these other kids who now 'belong' to you in certain situations. You need to give them more time and adjust your own expectations to a more realistic level. Let them cope with the schoolyard dynamics in their own way. It's unlikely that Suzie's children think your children are being rude, and children are very forgiving of one another, though perhaps your children do resent the relationship they have with you now. They may be aware of some ill-feeling on the part of their mum about your new partnership with another 'school parent', especially if she also goes to the school with them. If you think about their position, it really is quite complicated for them.

The best thing you could do to help them is probably not to try to discuss it with them, but rather to take steps to avoid putting your children in this awkward situation for the time being. However much you might want to carry on as if everything's fine, you should consider letting Suzie take her own children into school without you, or dropping them off outside and heading on. Only go in to deliver or pick up your own children, for the time being. This shows clearly who belongs to whom and, most importantly, which children are your priority. This will help them know how to behave and reassure them that you haven't abandoned them for Suzie's children.

'I have a new baby daughter now and my two boys aged eight and ten years old from my first marriage live with us and spend time with their father regularly. They love their new baby sister and the other day Jamie said: "Mum, can Emily come with us this weekend? We want to show her to Dad". I thought this was really nice, but I didn't know quite what to say!'

It's really touching that Jamie wanted to do this. It shows he wants to share his delight in his sister with his dad, rather than being afraid he has to keep his two families separate. For all sorts of reasons it obviously isn't appropriate that she goes, so welcome his remark for the affection it shows. Tell Jamie that Emily doesn't really belong in Dad's family the way he does, and that his time with Dad is special time for them to be together without other distractions, and add that she is too young to be away from you.

Sometimes new babies in any family give rise to sibling rivalry, which you've perhaps coped with before. This time there's an added element which is that Emily belongs to you and your new partner in a different way. The boys' father is somewhere else whereas their new sister's father is with her all the time. They will adjust to this OK but you can help by not drawing attention to this, especially when they're about to go off to see their father. So don't say, 'Emily belongs here, not with your dad' or 'We're going to be a family while you're gone'. Gently remind them of the boundaries between the two families, reinforcing their special relationship with their natural father, and showing your pride in their ability to go off on their own without you because they're older, whereas Emily has to stay at home.

'My older daughter has often said negative things about her stepfather, which worries me. You hear so much about step-fathers doing the wrong thing by their partners' daughters that I've become really concerned. If he truly is hard to get on with, I can't really keep encouraging her to be with her mum because this would surely make her feel unsupported, even betrayed, by me. Her mother, of course, wouldn't hear a word against him. I feel powerless to do anything. Josie is twelve years old and she's growing fast. Is there anything I can do?'

When Josie talks about her stepfather, do your best to really listen and take the conversation further by encouraging her to express herself, without your inquiries sounding too alarmed or inquisitive. Use the technique of asking her how she feels about her observations of him, without saying what you think or giving any leading questions. Ask her if she thinks her mum knows how she feels, and show you understand that it would probably be difficult for her to talk about it with her mum. It will help Josie if she feels she can speak to you and get her thoughts and feelings off her chest.

Acknowledge that it must be difficult for her that her mum has chosen a partner she doesn't seem to have taken to. Suggest that it may not matter if she doesn't particularly seek out his company, that she shouldn't feel she has to like him, that her own opinions are valuable. Remind her that we often have to find a way to relate to people we don't especially like and have to make some effort to get along despite these feelings. Explain how you obviously can't change anything to help her, that you regret the difficulties she is having, but her mother's choice of partner is clearly out of your hands. This will help you deal with feeling that you have to reinforce a relationship you have your own concerns about, the contradiction you're experiencing with Josie.

Don't let stereotypes about stepfathers cause you to imagine things. You haven't said you've heard anything from Josie to suggest that something improper may be the basis for her negativity. Keep in mind all the many more innocent reasons why a child may want to take a negative stand about a parent's new partner. Just because we hear a lot about child abuse these days it doesn't mean that most stepfathers are inclined to overstep proper boundaries for physical intimacy. But keep listening and consider trying to talk to her mother yourself about your observations.

'My ten-year-old son said the other day, "Mum doesn't like me talking about Sam and Julia". They are my wife's children, who mainly live with us. I said, "Well, you should if you want to!". How should I have dealt with this remark; was this reply OK?'

Your reply probably did no harm, but it would have been more helpful if you held back from replying in this way because it immediately contradicts a message he's getting from his mum. You could have said something more accepting like 'That's OK, I'm not bothered', not made any issue of the remark, and left it at that. Alternatively, you could have tried to work out the possible meaning behind the comment before assuming its basis was necessarily significant or even that it required attention. For instance, his mum may change the subject, because of her own feelings, when he mentions your children and he's noticed this. This is not the same thing as instructing him not to speak about them or that she disapproves of your stepfamily! She may have some anxieties about her son's enthusiasm for his time at your place, which she's trying to hide by avoiding talking about your new life, perhaps without even knowing she does this. Your son won't be disturbed by feeling he must opt not to mention them in order to please mum. This is a sensible way for him to deal with it. Many children seem to choose to keep their two families separate in their minds (as we saw earlier) and having these boundaries is a useful way of coping. It doesn't necessarily mean there are major secrets being hidden. You could say something like 'How do you feel about not talking about them?' and he'll probably reply with a reassuring 'It's no big deal, Dad'.

This is a good example of a situation where divorce business tends to make you supersensitive about your children's remarks. While it's true that your son should ideally be able to speak freely to his mum about anything, there's no point in asserting that to your child as a matter of principle, just because it irritates you that he can't. That just suggests right and wrong ways of doing things, as you see it, which isn't helpful for your son. So accept his way of dealing with it, and remember a lot of what you hear isn't worth worrying about except as an opportunity for mutually reinforcing dialogue.

'I was shocked by my teenage daughter's reaction when I told her recently I was getting married soon. I've been separated from her mother for some years now and we've enjoyed time together without any major problems. I've been keeping my relationship with my fiancée very much in the background until I was sure I wanted to tie the knot, because I was worried about how my former wife would react and I wanted to devote all my time to my children when we're together. Carly reacted angrily and

stomped out of the room in a bit of a state. I felt I'd done the wrong thing by her and I don't know quite how to break the ice between us.'

Your teenager seems to have reacted to the fact that a major decision you've made which will affect her has been announced, when she knew little about it. She resents this. Even younger children don't like family events being sprung upon them. They need time to get used to the idea and in the case of new partners, to get to know them in advance. Marriage seems very definite and permanent and Carly, because of your decision to keep your fiancée out of the picture, feels she was excluded from something important that's been happening to you which she would have liked to know about. Teenagers can be very sensitive and they can experience exclusions as put-downs when none were intended. Carly, as a teenager, is probably beginning to be quite concerned about love and relationships herself, so this is important stuff to her! All your children may be reacting with some uncertainty about how a new person is going to fit in with their time with you, and whether they will like her. Marriage means living together, so they know she will always be there as part of their family time with you, someone they haven't even met. All this is the reality of their position which, as usual, you need to get in touch with so you understand it.

As to salvaging the situation now that the news is on the table, you should call the children together and acknowledge that you realise the announcement seemed a bit sudden and that you're interested in their feelings about it. Tell them they are going to meet your partner soon and you plan to involve her in some of your family activities over the forthcoming weeks: see Chapter 4 regarding introductions. Say that you obviously like your fiancée a lot and that you very much hope they will come to like her too, in time. You're not implying that you needed their permission to marry, but that you now want to consider their reactions and involve them in the lead-up to living together.

This may solve the problem, but you may need to give your teenager a while to thaw out. Be patient. And don't forget to tell their mum yourself rather than leave the children to tell her this significant news. Don't be afraid to talk to your fiancée about your daughter's reaction, though you might be inclined not to, to avoid upsetting her. Later on it will be difficult for her if she can't understand her stepchildren's feelings because she doesn't know about them. Being able to discuss sensitive issues honestly will be a good start to your new stepfamily.

'Jamie told me the other day he had a fight with his stepbrother Tom. I'm worried that because Tom stays with his dad on the weekend that Jamie isn't with me, there's a problem with whether they're getting along. Should I say anything to Jamie's mum? How can I help Jamie? He's stuck with his mum having a new family and it must be hard for him.'

It isn't necessarily hard for Jamie just because *you* think it must be, although you're on the right track in trying to identify with his situation. Yes, he does have to try to accept Tom as that's the arrangement his mum has for her new partner's contact with his child. Jamie may have had a fight with his stepbrother but he's probably had many before with his schoolmates, which you didn't always hear about and which he probably coped with. He may report difficulties to you because they stick in his mind more than the pleasurable, easier times they have together. It's human nature to focus on negatives, which are hard to deal with, rather than on positives, which are never problematic!

Next time he's with you, ask him how he got on with Tom last weekend, and see what he says, without suggesting you expect there to have been more fights. If there have been, ask him why he thinks they happen, and listen. Ask him what he thinks might be a peaceful solution and try to help him work out a different approach with you. Tom may be wanting to assert his presence in his father's home, where Jamie spends a lot more time than he does, and his behaviour is a form of stepsibling rivalry. You obviously can't do anything about it, because it's for Tom's dad and Jamie's mum to deal with. But you can listen empathically and help Jamie with finding a way to deal with it, just as you would with any other kind of challenge he might bring to you. Again, remember that your protective parental concern is making you feel you need to do something because it's a separation-related issue, tending to make you attribute greater significance to it than is probably warranted. Also, don't forget to ask Jamie what was the *best* thing about the weekend Tom came to stay.

'My partner's children come and spend weekends with us, though their mum doesn't allow them to come as often as we'd like them to. Our combined families have a good time together once they've settled in, but I find they seem to say things to my children that sound competitive. Last weekend Joanne said to my daughter that her violin teacher was the best in town, implying that my daughter's music teacher wasn't as good. Another time she said, "This isn't my real home, you know!". I feel a need to protect my daughter and I'm irritated by these kinds of remarks. What should I say?'

It's a bit sad in one way that your visiting stepdaughter needs to assert herself like this. But in another way, you should remind yourself that making the occasional smart-alec remark or indulging in one-upmanship is something many children do, and we happily ignore it or make a light-hearted comment of some kind. However, in your situation it's understandable that you're irritated and this is probably because you feel that their mother might have put her up to it. This makes you feel upset about the position she has been put in, and how your daughter will cope with these comments. Remind yourself that children are often quite competitive by nature, and she might have said how well-qualified her music teacher is for quite innocent reasons. If these kinds of remarks tend to be made at the beginning of her time with you, they probably in part reflect her uncertainty about how she'll fit in with a family she's not part of all the time. I suggest you ignore it, or if you're all gathered together at the time, why not ask questions like 'How do you enjoy your lessons?', 'Where do you go for them?' or 'Does your teacher set you lots of practice?'. This way you've ignored the issue of who has the best teacher, but showed some interest in the topic raised. Encourage your daughter to volunteer something conversational about her music too.

The remark about where her real home is probably reflects some uncertainty about how she's supposed to behave and whether she'll get it right, which is to be expected. Her feelings about her two homes are likely to be a bit confused sometimes. I wouldn't worry about it unless you feel it upsets your child, who is the person she's speaking to. Then you could chip in with something like 'We hope you feel it's like a home while you're here' or something similarly low-key and reassuring. The remark isn't necessarily a negative comment — it may reflect her feelings that it *does* feel like a real home, or just that she wishes sometimes it *were* her 'real' one, etc.

Key Points for Successful Stepfamilies

Stepfamily life is so full of complexities that it's worth taking a detailed look at what to look out for and how to be ready for it. This will help you to communicate effectively with your children when issues arise.

- Acknowledge that your adult relationship has extra pressure to withstand, even though you both may have some family experience behind you. This time though, you didn't have a child-free period to consolidate your relationship without other demands on your time and your emotions; you weren't able to extend your family gradually. Each of you needs to feel secure about the strength of your relationship so you convey your solidarity as a couple to the children. They are more likely to accept and respect a step-parent who is a secure member of the partnership that heads the family.

- Establish a regular habit of talking about family issues as a couple. Don't be afraid to acknowledge your real feelings about family matters. Discuss how you think you'll each react to inevitable situations before they arise, such as how step-parents will feel about exercising authority when a 'natural parent' is absent. Work out a routine, such as calling a family conference, for settling family disputes before they get serious. Make a note of issues for later discussion when you're too busy to address them straight away.

- Take your time in adjusting to new relationships, remembering that there's nothing to say you must love your partner's children any more than you must love his sister or parents, though, of course, it does help if they're lovable at least sometimes! So don't expect your new partner to like your children automatically just because they're yours. Make sure your partner can talk about the children to you openly without worrying about your reactions to their honesty.

- If you're the one who's becoming a step-parent, don't expect clear-cut parental feelings about the children to emerge straight away, or to be accepted by the children immediately. Everybody's expectations of your role in the family (not to mention your own) will put pressure on you to adjust more quickly than is really feasible, so take each day at a time and accept that you will feel ambivalent about your new family quite often.

- Be prepared to handle some bad feelings about you from the stepchildren and even from your own children as they adjust to things. Try to acknowledge their feelings, but don't accept rudeness. Give some sensible detached guidance about relationships and feelings. These are real issues and it'll be worth the courage it sometimes needs to get things out in the open. As we've pointed out, they won't necessarily just take care of themselves.

- Do all you both can to foster your children's relationship with a largely absent parent. Your family is not wholly contained within your home, there is an influential adult elsewhere who is an ongoing part of your lives. The contact regime, whether it's children coming or children going, will sometimes seem like an intrusion and an inconvenience. But the children will adjust more quickly to their new family if their relationship with both their parents remains strong and they feel you support this, in your words as well as in your actions. This will only happen if everyone in the new family really feels positive about the children's permanent links with their past family.

- Being positive includes containing your inevitable frustrations in front of the children (owning your own feelings and dealing with them appropriately), avoiding comparisons, being interested (without being inquisitive) about their relationship with their absent parent and what they do together, not trying to take over all maternal or paternal responsibilities so the children feel you want to replace their parent, etc. Accept that you may have mixed feelings about the claim your stepchildren's absent parent has when you're doing all you can to provide a loving and nurturing new environment for them, along with all the hard work that involves. Be easygoing and accommodating about this aspect of family life, conveying that you accept it unquestioningly (even if you don't always), and seeing the advantages of it wherever you can.

- If you suspect that your children might actually enjoy their step-parent more than their 'real' parent, or become closer to them as time goes on, don't let this affect your positive approach to these two different relationships which you should try to see as complementary rather than in competition with each other. A child needs to feel free to form their own kind of bond with people who are important in their life.

- Don't make it too much of a special occasion too often when your own or your partner's children are with you. Convey that being all together is normal, as far as you're concerned. Let them fit into the family routine much as it is, at the same time making them feel they belong. Do some things that can involve everybody if the age range makes this feasible. This will help prevent children making comparisons about who is more important, as well as showing them life at your place as it really is.

- Make sure you each allow the other time alone with your biological children sometimes. This reinforces their special bond and gives you either time alone with your children or valuable time on your own.

- Resist the temptation always to intervene when you overhear comments that you think touch on sensitive issues. The children probably won't be as sensitive as you are and will ignore or forget them pretty quickly.

- When you hear reports of conflicts or arguments between stepsiblings, acknowledge that you'll feel protective of your own child, and any resentment you might harbour about your child having to get on with these other children will enhance this.

- Don't forget that children have to learn to negotiate their own peer relationships, and if they complain to you, you should respond with interest, support, some compassion and a little helpful advice about human relationships in general. In fact, respond just as you would to any friendship issue they might bring to you.

- Depending on the family history, half-siblings and stepsiblings can be as close as real brothers and sisters on an everyday basis. To avoid confusion and mixed messages, try to think of everyone as just a group of people getting on with life together.

- Don't be alarmed if they don't seem to get on after the initial novelty has worn off. They haven't chosen each other and may have had quite differ-ent upbringings. Expect there to be some tensions between the two sets of children. They don't have to like each other; they only have to adjust to each other so they can get along. If they are younger when you join forces, they probably will accept each other easily; this doesn't happen so readily with older children. However, do try to maintain standards, have fun, and don't feel you've always got to do everything together. Doing things separately can reinforce important family-of-origin bonds and groupings.

- Try not to treat the two sets of children differently in matters of discipline or favours. You're bound to feel differently about them, but aim for this not to show too much.

- Be confident, clear and consistent about your expectations of everybody, so everyone knows where they stand with you. Don't feel you always have to cover up feelings of frustration or rejection and alienation within the family. Express yourself and your needs accordingly, tuned accurately to the ages and feelings of the children and taking care not to be destructive or hurtful. And be sure you listen to and accept, though not necessarily encourage, the children's feelings and demands. Good luck!

CHAPTER 6

AUTHORITY, SECURITY AND EMOTIONAL FREEDOM

Your first thought is probably that this is going to be a chapter about discipline. Yes, that's part of it, but authority is really very much about a less obvious kind of leadership. It's about conveying confidence, being one step ahead of your children, conveying your own security and giving your children the right amount of choice about the right kinds of things. Authority, or the lack of it, is inherent in all our communications with children and so it's been part of all our suggested fielding strategies. Too much authority inhibits healthy experimentation, too little forces children to make decisions they aren't ready for, and this creates anxieties and insecurities, especially when it comes to separation issues.

There are two main reasons why parental authority is particularly important in today's families. The first has to do with our uncertainty about how to parent effectively nowadays. Much has been said lately in parenting manuals and social policy debates on the family about the crisis of confidence experienced by today's parents, and the importance of stable family structure as essential for healthy development. It's as if we may have become too liberal in reaction to so-called

'Victorian' restrictive parenting styles (the 'children should be seen and not heard' kind), most aspects of which we're well rid of! But just how are we supposed to be parents? How strict should we be nowadays?

We learn how to parent (just as we learn how to communicate) from how we ourselves experienced being parented. And yet society now is organised much more democratically than it was when our parents were children, learning about parenting from their parents. There was less uncertainty for parents raising children within a more authoritarian society. Much about those almost autocratic, repressive styles we wouldn't want to resurrect, but at least there was more of an implicit blueprint for what parents were supposed to do. Nowadays, however you have opted to bring up your children as far as discipline and authority are concerned, they are being educated in a significantly different, less disciplined environment where choices, cooperation, freedom of speech and right of reply are very much more encouraged.

This can make for a great deal of conflict in families, where there is obviously a need for some order and children need some structure and support in knowing what is expected of them. But how much? Children from a young age feel free to resist parental attempts at control, expect to speak their minds and be listened to. They are encouraged to feel they have a say in almost everything in the interests of encouraging free expression and experimentation, and children's rights are a constant focus for community attention, in most ways rightly so. But we have not as parents had much help in how to preserve the right amount of authority within families in the context of this kind of society. Many of us believe in a laissez-faire type of parenting, thinking we are being modern and liberal, and then we wonder why our children are not more cooperative, helpful and obedient! It's as if we may have set them free to take responsibility for their lives and their actions before they are emotionally ready for such freedom. We've probably all experienced the frustrating backlash of allowing, against our better judgment, our children to stay up late because they seemed to want to, and then having to face the consequences of undone homework, morning lateness, bad tempers and wishing we'd been more assertive about appropriate bedtimes!

The second reason why parental authority is particularly important in today's families is that separating has a way of causing parents to be extra doubtful about how to manage their children. Doing it on your own, however much you feel you were unsupported during your marriage in recent times, is different. You may be struggling with difficult emotions yourself and feeling a failure as a partner. Financially, things may be rather uncertain. You may be feeling guilty and tempted to overindulge your children in order to compensate for what you've subjected them to. If you spend less time with your children now and you've not had much experience being solely in charge of them, you may be tentative about being too dominant for fear of putting them off their time with you, and because you don't want to spoil your limited time together with frequent confrontations. All these factors tend to undermine your confidence in yourself as a person, and also as a parent. For a period after a separation many parents experience disorganisation, lack of confidence and inconsistency in their parenting while everyone is adjusting to all the changes, and this is just when your children most need the security of confident, firm and positive parenting.

Authority contributes crucially to your children's security and emotional freedom. To understand this, it helps to think

again about what as parents we want for our children. We want them to grow up free to experiment confidently but safely with the world around them and acquire skills which enhance their self-image so they maximise their potential. As we noted in Chapter 1, we tend to think of caring for our children's welfare in terms of food, shelter, love, health, education, exercise, continuity of family care, etc.

Communicating with the right amount of authority ensures your child is sure enough about themself to benefit from the provision of those practical things and has the emotional freedom to reach their potential. 'Emotional intelligence', the ability to understand and constructively express your emotional temperament, to use a new phrase, is increasingly being recognised as a more important predictor of successful life than all the A grades you can collect. If you can't get on with people, being brilliant may not get you anywhere because very few people can be happy in social isolation. If you try to deny anxiety because you don't want to admit you experience it, you won't be able to be an effective public speaker, however valuable what you have to say is!

Encouraging our children to be free agents too early in their lives can contribute to a sense of aimlessness and uncertainty, and an inability to use opportunities constructively. Appropriate limit-setting with emotional guidance (see also Chapter 7) is crucial to the development of potential. The solid anchor of a guiding and interested family base is very necessary for today's young people.

Separation can be a threat to a child's security and emotional development. Therefore, here we're going to show further how important authority is for giving your child emotional freedom to continue important relationships after separation and to feel secure about significant family changes.

'I find that on Sunday evenings my two children don't want to pack up to go back to their mum's. The truth is that I'm sad they have to go and it's hard to be too strict with them. How should I handle this?'

You should be calm but firm, and leave plenty of time to get organised so there isn't a last-minute rush and tension becomes associated with having to go back to Mum's. This is obviously harder when you don't want them to have to go. Perhaps you're afraid they'll think you really want them to go if you're too enthusiastic about getting organised. Their reticence doesn't necessarily mean they don't want to go; it probably only means they'd rather continue with what they're doing. Leaving after a happy weekend is sad for you all. But don't forget that everybody loves the freedom of weekend leisure time, and to some degree thinking about the week ahead and getting back into weekday routine wouldn't be something they wanted to think about even if you were all still together! Wanting to stay with you doesn't mean not wanting to be with their mum (see also Chapter 3), though sometimes parents react as if it might be this.

You can recognise that it's a pity they have to pack up because the weekend's over and you're sad they have to go. But you should also reassure them that you'll be fine (they shouldn't feel they are responsible for your sadness and have to worry about it) and you're looking forward to next time. They need your calm authority very much so that the changeover is made easier and so that they sense your confidence in the arrangements and don't have to take too much responsibility themselves, especially if they're young. This conveys that you are in charge of your parenting responsibilities, as you should be. Try giving them a ten-minute warning signal about packing up and starting to get ready. If their hesitancy means you're running late, it may inconvenience or irritate their mum and she may make a comment in front of them when you arrive, or phone you to ask where you've got to. Even if you think she should be more accepting and laid-back about timing, it's best to avoid opportunities for her to express irritation which will be transmitted to the children. You can pre-empt this by giving her a call to confirm timing. Try to think of this not as bowing and scraping to your ex, but rather as showing respect for other people's positions, a good message for your children. It also tells them you're in charge of the arrangements arising from the separation. It's surprising how many parents get caught up in accusing each other of not keeping to agreed schedules over quite small time variations, when they wouldn't even comment or worry if it was a friend who had taken the children out and was running late.

'I sometimes have to pull my wife's young children into line and I wonder what I should do about the "You're not my real dad!" kind of retort I sometimes get. Of course, it's true, but it's a pretty clear statement that they don't want to accept my authority. Any ideas?'

This is a classic situation and you need to think about their position, take their apparent rejection of your authority with a grain of salt and not let it get to you! Don't be afraid that asserting yourself may generate unfavourable comparisons with their dad, or that they will reject you generally. They may be testing you out. Although as parents we don't like insubordination, we must recognise that for children, adjusting to another adult (and therefore an authority figure) takes some time. You aren't their dad, and you probably are different from him. They're noticing this. They may still be harbouring some resentment of your position in their mother's life, and they feel like flexing their muscles towards you momentarily. Alternatively, they don't want to cooperate and this is the first way out they thought of; it was just a method of arguing their way out of doing something they didn't want to do.

You should firmly, but not fiercely — this shows they've got under your skin! — say that in your house you are often responsible for decisions about them. Say that you expect them to comply, and quietly insist. Don't be tempted to discuss their dad and how he may assert authority, because this involves them in a comparison of your relative status in their lives, as if your authority with them is negotiable; anyway it's irrelevant because he isn't there at the relevant time — *you* are in loco parentis. Remind them that you've all got to get on together and that their mum has appointed you as her second-in-charge. Don't give in to them because you want them to like you. Talk to their mum and get her support for the role you are assuming with them. If the problem persists, call a family conference and repeat your expectations of them, while, as usual, listening to their comments.

It might also be worth having a look at what kinds of demands you make on them. Perhaps you're not all that used to having children around, and you often want to keep them at arm's length. You may have some adjusting to do too!

'There are certain things my children do which I disapprove of, like insisting that they should be allowed to watch endless television shows, not wanting to go to bed, making objections about what I suggest we do together, and I find this hard. I don't want our limited time together to be full of confrontations, or have them tell me what Mum lets them do as if I'm being too strict.'

You must stay in charge of the rules you want to have in your household. If you give in too often you'll find it much harder to toughen up later when you (and maybe your new partner) are increasingly letting the household be run by the children and you're feeling frustrated and irritable. It's very tempting to indulge your children against your better judgment when you're nervous about too many confrontations. Be confident in firmly restating the rules you want respected, without referring to the rules they live under anywhere else. Call a meeting next time they're with you and discuss what activities you will do together. Suggest everyone takes turns — including you — in choosing what you all do. And don't forget that children often object to things that you know they'll enjoy, so be masterful and insist cheerfully! Don't be put off too easily by sulks and protests, they'll soon move on and get into whatever you've got in store. Be prepared to put aside time to help them amuse themselves, preferably with you actually involved, as an alternative to endless television if you think they watch too much: see also Chapter 1.

'My fourteen-year-old daughter and I often have arguments and she flounces off and goes over to her dad's. She wants to have the key to his place and I won't let her because I don't think she should have this kind of exit option just because she isn't getting her own way. I know she thinks her father is less strict with her than I am. But, of course, he thinks I'm just trying to obstruct their relationship.'

Everybody knows about confrontations with teenagers; your daughter is struggling with wanting her own independence. You seem to know that withdrawing from confrontations is not a good way of handling them in the long term. Offer her plenty of opportunities to go to her dad's when things are calm, but insist that she stay and talk it through with you, using all the listening and identifying techniques we've described elsewhere. Try to have a talk with her dad about how you want to deal with her and see if you can get him to recognise that it's important you now conduct your respective relationships with her as separate ones, though you'd like him to reinforce your approach to limit-setting. Try to get him to agree that she doesn't go to his place unless you have agreed to this. Reassure yourself that it's quite common for teenagers to manipulate the divided family situation to suit themselves. They are attracted to regimes which they think give them more freedom, often before they are emotionally ready to use that freedom constructively. And it's common for Mum to have more of the rule-enforcing times with her children, when discipline is more often necessary, while Dad has the children during weekends and holidays, when things can be more relaxed. There's more about communicating with teenagers in Chapter 8.

'I think it's up to the children when they want to spend time with their father. I don't want to stop them from going, but they don't seem to want to. My husband is threatening to take me to court because he's only seen them once since we separated. He should have thought of the children when he decided to leave us. How should I be dealing with this? They are five and eight years old and their dad was never much involved with them when we were together. I don't think he really cares about them.'

You shouldn't leave it to your children to 'decide' whether they want to see a loved parent, as we've mentioned elsewhere. In the predicament they're in they can't possibly make an independent choice. It's probably difficult for you to see this if you feel inside that he abandoned all three of you. He can't be feeling this if he is trying to see them, and it's important that whatever *you* feel, your children don't feel deserted by him. You are unwittingly communicating to your children that it is OK not to see him, and probably also that you don't really want them to want to. Ask yourself whether you are subconsciously sabotaging their freedom to be with him because of your own need to punish him for leaving. You may not want to think you're doing this, but consider the messages you are giving out. The children's apparent lack of interest may well reflect their need to secure your goodwill and identify with your position, at the expense of their own freedom to enjoy their father's interest in them. They don't necessarily feel the same as you do about him.

What they need is for you to be more authoritative about arrangements and to hear you really be committed and enthusiastic about them spending time with him. Until they do, they will not feel able to be enthusiastic about Dad themselves, and you will be inhibiting them emotionally from a relationship they have a right to enjoy despite your feelings. It's annoying for you that he wants them now when you think he didn't contribute before. He was probably withdrawing more and more from family life because of his feelings about the marriage. You should try to adjust your attitude to being able to see that they have needs that are separate to yours, and that even if he didn't appear to show much interest in them before, as far as their long-term wellbeing is concerned it's better that they enjoy his interest now than never.

Hard though it may sound, you can't be the one to decide whether he's interested in his children. The children have a right to contact with their father.

You should ask him when and how often he wants to see them and get some regular arrangement going soon which you think might suit you. Then sit them down, tell them that you and Dad have decided on a plan and that from now on it's going to happen this way. Do the very best you can to be positive about it and show them you want it for them. You could say something like: 'You're sure to find you have fun; sometimes people hesitate and miss out on happy things. We all have to do things we think we'd rather not occasionally, so off you go, I'm happy for you to be seeing your dad!'. This is cheerfully confident, and sympathetic but firm in its message. This is the low-key but assertive, positive approach we suggested in Chapter 3 that you use when children seem hesitant. It is appropriately authoritative.

If you're worried that you may let yourself down in front of them at handover, and communicate something unhelpful, why not suggest he picks them up from school when they are seeing him? Then you won't have to see him and the children will have had a neutral interval between time with each of their parents.

'I'm quite recently separated and our son is only sixteen months old. He's always been in my full-time care. His dad is being very difficult and says he wants to take over his care. Josh is spending Sundays with his dad but the pickups are difficult, because his dad seems to want to prove Josh doesn't need me. The other morning he had Josh in his arms and I said to Josh, "Give Mummy a kiss goodbye", and he wouldn't. His dad said, "See, he doesn't want to!". I felt really undermined.'

This is a situation you need to take charge of, because you can do things to avoid this kind of opportunity for Josh's father to be unhelpful and to upset you. First, console yourself that the episode probably didn't mean too much to Josh, although he would have sensed the tension between you and if this becomes prolonged it's obviously not good for him. So instead of asking something of your child in this awkward situation, something he can't give, take charge yourself. Before you pass him to his father, say, 'Mummy's going to say goodbye now', and give him a big kiss and a cuddle from you.

'I'm finding I'm quite often the one to make decisions about things like how late my stepdaughter, who is fifteen years old, should stay out and how much weekend spending money she should have, because her father is not around at the time. I tend to hesitate about what line to take and we end up discussing it for ages. It doesn't help that I'm quite a lot younger than her mother. How strict should I be?'

You should have a definite policy worked out and stick to it. We're often tempted to talk things through so as to try to be fair and explain our reasons, but this tends to communicate that the issue is negotiable when it isn't. The result can be ongoing debates aimed at wearing you down, which are debilitating and undermining to your self-confidence. In your case it doesn't help that you're the stepmother, so you're less sure of your ground. Couple solidarity is extra important in stepfamilies, where the lines of authority are a bit blurred. Talk to her father and form a plan. Meet together and present what you have agreed to your stepdaughter, and then refer clearly and firmly to the agreed policy when situations crop up. Try not to be too aware of the age gap. Remember you are in partnership with her father, who has delegated certain matters to you, though most of the time you probably feel like friends, and she may not want to 'take orders' from you or from anyone, being a typical teenager!

One of the traps for parents who want to listen to their children and have them understand the reasons for their rules is that they invite negotiation accidentally. Look at your language, and don't fall into the trap of explaining yourself to younger children, because they probably won't understand, or even want to listen. They want whatever it is *now*! If you're not sure, say you want to think about it for a moment and get back to them, perhaps after you've discussed it with Mum (or Dad). But don't be afraid to say no, and add that you are responsible for their welfare, and that's your decision, full stop. Many parents are quite easily undermined by their children's verbal onslaughts, and are uneasy about pulling rank. This is a manifestation of our uncertainty about how to parent nowadays, which we discussed earlier in this chapter. Children need you to be firm about many issues, in order to feel secure that you're there with their interests at heart, even though they may protest vigorously. Use authority firmly but without raising your voice, as this can be frightening to young children especially, and the debate can become an undignified contest over who can shout the loudest!

'I have two sons aged seven and nine years old who spend week-ends fortnightly with their father. He seems to buy them a lot of things whenever they ask him. I don't agree with this and it seems sad that this is how they see him, as a treasure chest! How should I handle this?'

You should assert unhesitatingly your way of dealing with requests to be bought things. Say something along the lines of 'I'm not getting you this today, but remember that when it's your birthday I'll be listening for ideas!'. If you get a protest, just say no. They have to know you are different from their father and have different ways of parenting.

Have the courage of your convictions and gently explain that buying them things all the time isn't your style. Don't say you can't afford it; you sound as if you don't believe in too much material indulgence anyway and so this excuse would miss the point. Stick to your convictions, without implying that they could have whatever it is they want if you had as much money to spend on them as Dad seems to. Your treats will have a lot more impact and last longer in their minds. And remember, children, exposed as they are to peer and advertising pressures, can seem very materialistic, so try to see their demands in the context of these pressures. Maybe yours feel they can somehow connect with their father this way, which may have its place.

Don't let his different way of doing things undermine you. Your love and consistent firmness will stand them in very good stead. Their needs for security will be served by you being firm about setting limits on their demands, even though they may momentarily resent not getting their own way.

Key Points for Staying in Charge

- Don't give children too much choice about the arrangements for seeing each of their parents in your effort to be open and liberal: see Chapter 3. Effective authority is being able to make your children feel listened to, without them thinking they're deciding things — especially separation matters — themselves. Later on, when they're more used to the separation and are getting older, is the time to involve them more in any negotiations.

- Try to reinforce the idea that you and their other parent are still able to communicate and be a team about their welfare, by talking together about

---

matters that should still concern you both. This conveys an important message about continued parental authority and responsibility.

- Give clear, positive messages about the importance of their other parent as interested and available to them for consultation and guidance.

- Be confident that you can make good decisions for your children at this difficult time, and be prepared to be decisive, even if you modify your approach later.

- Give children plenty of notice about major changes you may have in store for them, so they have time to get used to them, and feel involved in family goings-on.

- Don't be too hard on yourself if you find you're not feeling completely in charge at times. Think about what was going on and how you may have appeared to the children; then call a family meeting, acknowledge that you weren't at your best that day and tell them what you now expect of them. In other words, tell them you want a 'rerun'!

- Children forget things and often don't think things through. They're learning all the time and are often very impatient and impulsive. Don't be afraid to reiterate the rules of your household from time to time so they know what you expect of them.

- Don't be tempted, as we've said elsewhere, to relax discipline because of a separation. Children need the security of rules, limits and standards.

- Don't forget to give praise and appreciation when your children do things on time, without resistance or protest, so that you reinforce and give attention to helpful behaviour more than you pay attention to unhelpful behaviour. Being difficult can become a child's way of getting much-needed parental attention if you don't attend enough to cooperative behaviour.

- Assert your authority firmly, clearly and patiently. Children want to endear themselves to you, so there's every chance this will work. Consult a parenting manual if you are looking for new ways of staying in charge because yours don't seem to be working.

CHAPTER 7

ABOUT FAULT, TRUTH AND FEELINGS

Like anyone else, children want reasons for things in order to make sense of their world. You'll no doubt remember when your youngsters went through that stage of asking endless questions about everything! Children especially want to make some kind of sense of the way their family has turned out; they may feel they want to apportion blame themselves to make sense of their parents' split-up. By hearing things said by their parents about each other, they may be put in a position of needing to know the 'truth' and to adopt a position themselves. This often seems like having to make a judgment about one parent at the expense of the other. Some parents engage in enlisting their children in setting the record straight about the facts of the break-up. This, of course, places the children in a position of needing to love and feel loved by someone who is at fault according to their other loved parent: an impossible conflict of loyalties! Even when you're trying hard to protect them from becoming engaged in what's going on between you and your partner, the emotions you're experiencing will give out some kind of message that you're not getting on, which will, of course, unsettle them and make them wonder which of you is causing the most hurt. How children make sense of and somehow survive the contradictory, even competitive, messages they may get from each of their parents is a credit to their resilience, though they obviously have little choice but to cope somehow.

Some parents are surprised at their children's apparent lack of interest in what is going on and absence of questions. This doesn't necessarily mean they don't have questions or concerns, or that they don't care and aren't finding things difficult. It often means they're anxious not to take sides and want to remain neutral and fair about it all, or they don't know how to give expression to their confused and uncertain feelings, or even whether they should do so. Separation brings about intense feelings in people. Children can experience quite profound sadness, intense anger, and anxiety at different times, which they may have difficulty expressing.

Fault and blame

Modern no-fault divorce law reinforces the view that relationship breakdown is a two-way process; that neither party is more to blame than the other. In our efforts to reinforce our children's positive regard for both their parents we try to cover up the contributions to the breakdown that each has made, and keep our adult arguments private. But wrongs *are* committed and keeping a stiff upper lip is not always entirely helpful to children. They need to know something of what their parents do to each other, but should hear it from them in such a way that they're clear they're not responsible for adult faults and that they aren't involved directly themselves. Getting this right is a difficult task. Minimising the extent to which you involve your children in conflicts of loyalty about who was to blame is your responsibility. Fielding their questions skilfully is how you do it, though, of course, you can't do much about what messages they're getting from their other parent unless you're still able to meet and discuss what line to take about your past together. Even when they don't seem to be asking their own questions of you, giving out the right amount of information and explanations from time to time also helps them.

It's important that children feel they can refer to what happened between you, that it's not a taboo subject because they sense you're reluctant to discuss it. They may decide that what you aren't telling them must be something really awful if it has to be secret. Keep your answers to questions they may raise from time to time simple. Don't forget there are certain things children can't be expected to understand because they are very adult or complex, such as the notion of romantic love, that not loving someone any more doesn't mean you hate them and how people who care for each other can do hurtful things, etc. So don't be tempted to volunteer too much in the way of explanations. Young children especially cannot begin to understand the affairs of adults, and you will risk making them confused and anxious if you try too hard to let them know what happened. You'll remember we talked about this in Chapter 2, in reference to when you are preparing to break the news about your separation. If you managed to handle this reasonably well, your children should feel comfortable about bringing up the topic from time to time as questions arise and new events take place.

'I found it very difficult when my teenage daughter came to me and asked me whether it was true that when I was away on business a couple of years ago I was seeing a particular lady friend. I wanted to be honest with her about why her mum and I separated, but I didn't want to tell her that I'd done the wrong thing while we were still together. Our marriage at that time was

pretty well over for me but my new partner wasn't the reason. I wouldn't have been interested in someone else if I'd been happy in my marriage. If I'd told my daughter the truth, I would have been blamed for betraying the marriage, and doing the wrong thing by her mother. It's a lot more complex than this so it's hard to know what to say!'

If you did begin your relationship with this person while you were still in the marriage, you must decide what you want your daughter to know from you, when you may not know what her mother has told her. You may know that the real story contradicts the kind of standards about marriage you want to be teaching your children. Many a parent has to face dealing with not matching the standards they set for their children! It's probably better that you recognise you were at fault than to imply that what you did was OK by evading the question or lying, when your daughter may know there was someone else for you while you and her mother were still together.

Accept her question and invite her to tell you what sort of concerns gave rise to it, so you explore her feelings with her. Why not try to turn her question into a heart-to-heart with her about relationships and blame? Say something about how new relationships can seem interesting when things aren't right at home, but that it's fairer all round to put those possibilities aside and concentrate on addressing the problems in the marriage (if you believe this, that is). Ask her what she thinks about this. If it's true that you were keeping company with your friend well before your separation it's probably best to tell her. She must learn about your 'failings' some time, and that people sometimes do behave in a way which is contrary to their expressed beliefs and values. If it's not true, as you did know of this lady during your marriage but didn't start seeing her romantically until after you separated, and don't think she was the cause of the split, then tell your daughter this. Her mum may well want to continue to believe you were cheating on her, so you can say you understand if mum feels you did the wrong thing by her, which you regret. You could add that separation always involves different points of view about how things were, and often doesn't bring out the best in people. See if she can tell you how she feels about your explanation, and accept it if she needs to blame you or feels disappointed in you. Having things out in the open is always better than avoiding a topic.

'Last weekend my small daughter, aged five years, said that Mum had told her I took their television! I was furious because as far as I was concerned her mother had agreed about what I should take when I left, and they've got the big-screen set. It doesn't help that my wife has our home and is really very well provided for. It felt as if my daughter thought I'd stolen it! I had to tell her it wasn't true.'

You needed to think on your feet despite your irritation. The moment may have passed, but here's what you could have said; maybe you can refer back to the episode and help your daughter. Consider her position before you contradict what she said, because that leaves her not knowing who's right and who's wrong, an uncomfortable dilemma she shouldn't have to deal with. It's an adult issue, albeit a relatively trivial one concerning an appliance. Her mum may not have accused you outright of taking something from them. Your daughter may have noticed that they were one television short, asked about it and Mum said, perhaps with some bitterness about the separation in general, that you took it. She may have implied to your daughter in the way she said it that you took it deviously without her consent or knowledge.

Whatever gave rise to your daughter's accusing question to you, you should aim to 'lift' the burden of her having to sort out what happened between you and her mum off her five-year-old shoulders. Scoop her up affectionately and say something like: 'Mum and I had to work out what we're all going to need, and I thought the TV was OK with her. Maybe Mum's feeling a bit sad, as we all are sometimes about dividing things up. I'm sure she doesn't really mind too much. I'll sort it out with her if there's been a misunderstanding'. Or you could say, 'I don't see it quite like that, not as stealing, but we sure do have a few things still to sort out, don't we?'. Then change the subject, or even enjoy switching on and watching the television together. You may be furious that your ex-wife has put you in a bad light, but don't show it. You need to convey that you aren't phased by her remark, that it isn't your daughter's problem, and that you aren't going to be drawn into a contest about the truth, or criticise Mum for what you think she said. However, you've offered a forgiving acknowledgment of what might have been said, and showed you listened to her.

With an older child you could consider saying something like: 'Maybe because when we split up I was the one who moved, it does feel as if I'm taking things that she'd rather keep because she'd prefer we hadn't separated. I'd rather we'd been able to work things out too, but dividing things up sensibly and fairly is what has to happen and we'll go on trying to sort it out'. This communicates uncritically how you see it and gives your child a useful angle on feelings she can reflect on while she works out how to deal with it in her own way.

'My twelve-year-old daughter asked me recently while visiting why her mother and I had separated. The real truth is that I couldn't live with her mother's sexual apathy and lack of

*affection any longer so I left her. Then later I found out she'd
been having an affair. I don't think it's fair for a child not to know
the truth, especially if hiding it from her puts me in a bad light. So
I told her her mother had been cheating on me.'*

It may seem a bit late now (though not too late to have another conversation with her) but before you go into detailed
reasons for the break-up, ask yourself why you needed to set
the record straight with your child by involving her in adult
business (and therefore in loyalty conflicts) which she can't
possibly understand. Remember your differences and frustrations are adult business and you are a parent — your child
shouldn't have to feel sorry for you, or be on the receiving end
of criticisms coming from one person she loves about another
she loves. If your wife's affair is past and gone, you could have
left it unmentioned and a matter for her to talk about with
your daughter if she wants to. Did you really want her to know
the truth because 'you shouldn't lie to children', or were you
really wanting her to know who's right and who's wrong as
you see it, because that's only fair? Or did you want to salvage
your reputation with your child? Think about the difference
between these and come up with an honest answer! Marital
faults are committed, but both of you share the responsibility
for how you dealt with them.

One suggestion for your situation is to refer back to her
question and say you've been thinking about it and you'd like
to say some more about it. For example: 'Mum and I had some
problems between us which we couldn't resolve. Each of us
dealt with it in our own different way. For some time I felt she
wasn't showing me any affection, which made me feel neglected
and unhappy. I decided we had to separate. Your mum found
someone else although I didn't know it at the time. Doing that
was her decision, though it did hurt my feelings'. This is how it

was and you're showing your daughter you're prepared to recognise Mum's position. Remember the conflict of loyalty your version of the 'truth' may involve your children in. Practise ways you can answer questions which avoid blaming, without actually lying.

Remember, in working out what to say to your children always consider how it's likely to come across to them. The tone of voice and emphasis you use will very much affect how much blame and bitterness the content of your words conveys. Put yourself in their shoes so you communicate empathically. They are attached to and emotionally dependent on both you and their mum, so test out in your own mind first the likely impact on them of what you think you want to say. This will guide you.

'I was really angry the other day when my nine-year-old daughter Julia said to me, "Mum says I can't have new shoes, she can't afford them because you don't give her enough money". I pay her mum a lot of money towards the children's expenses and I know she spends a lot on clothes for herself and holidays. I said it wasn't true that I didn't give her mum enough money. Surely she shouldn't be saying this sort of thing to the children?'

Well, no, she shouldn't, but she probably did say something at some stage about being short of money which gave rise to your daughter's accusation. Perhaps she is frustrated about aspects of her separated situation and all the adjustments she is having to make. Maybe she does think she has the lion's share of all the difficult decisions and expenses. She may be feeling anxious about her finances if you were the major family bread-winner, and she may sometimes resent the fact that you're now spending money on your own life separate from your former family. In other words, think about the context of your child's remark.

You should say something open-ended and blame-free to your child, rather than 'it isn't true', which involves them in questions about who is right and who is wrong (as we've said before). Explain that 'finances between Mum and I have been difficult to work out and sometimes things might not seem fair'. Ask her how she feels about not getting new shoes — allowing her the opportunity to express herself to you and identify her feelings. Say that finances are a bit different now and you all have to work out what's the most important thing to be spending money on. We live in a very materialistic culture, and you could help deflect your child's apparent resentment by taking the conversation further into whether having things that you think you want, such as new clothes, CDs, etc., makes you happy except for a brief moment. You will have listened to your child's remark without discussing with her the rights and wrongs of adult business, and opened her mind to new interpretations of her situation. You could ask her to suggest that Mum talks to you about any strains on the budget or, preferably with a nine-year-old, tell her that you will talk to her mum soon. Even though you may be sure Mum doesn't have a case, this reinforces the idea that finances are adult business the children should not have to feel caught up in, although their mum may be angry with you.

Major marital faults

You can't always gloss over the reality that there have been unpleasant arguments, drunkenness, overt affairs, etc. Trying to pretend that family life is rosy when it clearly isn't is more confusing than facing events squarely and helping your children come to terms with having a less than ideal family in a way that helps prevent them blaming themselves.

Very young children are best protected from full knowledge of sometimes frightening marital behaviour and, anyway, are much less likely to ask for explanations or reasons. They will usually quite readily accept a simple explanation that conceals difficult realities. Older children will often know about such behaviour, but it's still best for them if you can talk to them in terms of your having decided reluctantly that the marriage is better finished because it obviously isn't working with these things going on repeatedly; or that, yes, you or Mum has done wrong and hurtful things.

Field their questions — according to their age and comprehension level — about who's to blame, by saying things like: 'Sure it's destructive to be violent, drunk, unfaithful [etc.], but different people deal with situations in different ways, and sometimes people do behave badly to people they love and care for. It doesn't make sense, but it happens'. If applicable, you could say: 'Yes, I'm very much to blame. Marriages are difficult to get right and hard to understand, but we both care for you even if we can't care for each other'. When you think about it, you are both 'to blame' for the separation even when one of you has committed the obvious faults, because one of you is responsible for the damaging behaviour and the other decided it was unacceptable rather than continuing to put up with it.

This method of taking the particular and turning it into the general is a useful and reassuring way of fielding children's questions, as we've shown elsewhere. Instead of dwelling on the downright blameworthiness of one of their parents, you still acknowledge the behaviour but you do it by referring to the difficulty and hurtfulness of aspects of human nature sometimes, especially within relationships. Also, you can give a clear message that you are brave enough to take the step of refusing to put up with continued bad treatment, even if this means separating is the only solution for you.

Be prepared to accept that the children probably need to blame someone, whether they show this or not. Younger children especially will be inclined to blame you if you're the one moving out. Accept this blame without arguing about its validity, affirming your commitment to them despite the faults they're wanting to attribute to you. And try to explain that whoever moved out was not abandoning them, while accepting that they might feel this, so you show you understand their position. Tell them it just made most sense in the short term for you to be the one who moved.

Feelings

Most people have difficulty expressing feelings accurately or appropriately. We all know about stiff upper lips, spitting the dummy, hidden agendas, mixed messages, etc.: see Chapter 1. Sometimes we don't even know what we feel about an issue or a situation. We get into all sorts of muddles by not communicating our feelings accurately. However, emotional literacy, or the lack of it, is thankfully receiving lots of attention in personal growth circles.

Men are charged with being the ones who have most difficulty in expressing certain kinds of feelings such as tenderness, anxiety and fear. Women are often uneasy about expressing anger and being assertive. We learn (or fail to learn) about our emotional character and appropriate outlets for its expression from our family of origin, particularly our parents, as said earlier. However, although we may feel confused and incompetent in this area ourselves, we must try to give our children some guidance. Feelings belong to the person experiencing them and they need to be expressed somehow, without unduly influencing others. Anger and sadness tend to be the most difficult feelings to deal with, the ones we think of as negative. We tend to react automatically to people's anger and sadness as if they should be calmed down or cheered up as soon as possible. Sometimes people do feel sad and angry with good reason and we don't always need to react as if these feelings should be got rid of; the expression of feelings appropriate to the circumstances is healthy and necessary. As parents we tend to feel responsible for our children's feelings and often react to them as if we've got to find a solution ourselves. This is especially so when we think they are separation-related feelings. But we need to help children to learn how to deal with their feelings themselves rather than impose our own restrictions on their expressions of emotion.

'John was telling me the other night when I was trying to settle him to sleep peacefully that at Dad's place he sometimes gets scared. I asked him what Dad did about it and he said his dad ignores him, won't read him a story and just tells him to go to sleep. I hate to think of John being upset and feeling neglected. I didn't really know what to say so I just did what I always do to ensure the day ends peacefully: we spent some time talking.'

Most mothers would be concerned at what sounds like Dad's heartless approach, and worry that John is neglected. They'd feel anger and protective outrage, and may be anxious that something at Dad's place is causing the fears and uneasiness. They would think: why can't he see what John needs? Mum can do absolutely nothing to change estranged Dad's parenting practices, but she can reassure and support her child so that he can deal with the situation better when he is next at Dad's.

The helpful, non-judgmental way to deal with John's remarks is, first, to sympathise, giving validity to his remarks without showing too much concern, so he feels listened to. You were spot-on in inviting John to tell you how he tries to deal with the situation. You could say, for example: 'That must have upset you a bit, it sounds as if you needed comforting; did you get to sleep in the end?'. Then say something like 'Well done for being brave and managing OK', which communicates your confidence in him. Then you might explain how different people do things differently, and add, 'Maybe Dad thinks you're tough enough to look after yourself, or maybe he didn't realise you were upset partly because you didn't want him to know [etc.]'. Then get on (as you did) with whatever things you know work to settle him down or comfort him. Encourage him to feel it's OK to tell Dad what he needs and what will help him.

Depending on how well you get on with Dad, you could mention your concern about John not settling down at night (even if he always does with you), and see if he has trouble getting him peacefully settled. Then you can maybe tell him what you find works. This is about as close as you can go towards telling him how he should be managing John. Remember, young children are often unsettled when away from home and Mum. It probably doesn't mean anything serious, or that he can't manage. If he were feeling this way at a school camp you'd probably never get to hear about it, and if you did you'd probably know exactly what to say; you'd assume it was just a chance episode and not worry unduly. Dealing with these kinds of challenges is an important part of growing up. Parents, and mums in particular, tend to want to rescue their children from minor distresses which, in fact, they can learn useful things from by handling them in their own way. Perhaps John was just appreciating Mum's comforting presence, rather than complaining about his dad's approach.

Late in the day is often a time when children have difficult-to-field emotional outpourings and show intense behaviours. It's partly due to fatigue. Ceasing activities and winding down before sleep creates an empty 'mind-space' ready to be filled with things! Sometimes children may seem inconsolable, and you may be tempted to read all sorts of divorce-related bogies into their behaviour. They are active, growing fast all the time and their emotions sometimes get the better of them.

Late-night tantrums are very wearing, but try to use validating remarks like 'I can see you're very upset about this'. Don't make the mistake of trying to reason with them when they're being irrational. It may break your heart to be unable to settle them down but if it doesn't work, say a firm good night and leave them to it. If they protest about you leaving the room, insist that you're going to go, but that you'll come back in fifteen minutes to see how they are. They'll probably be asleep when you return, and will have forgotten about it the next morning. You can reassure yourself by referring back to the episode and ask if they feel OK about last night's upset now — they'll probably have moved on, and may even say, 'Sorry Mum!'. Male children in particular get conditioned to 'keep it all in' from an early age, so it has to come out at night when they're tired, and Mum is the person they feel OK with about showing their 'wussy' doubts, fears and tears. Late at night is also when you're least equipped yourself for dealing with confused and upset junior ramblings, so they're particularly trying! Don't be too self-critical if you don't think you handled a situation as effectively as you'd have liked to. Emotional expressions are hard to deal with and there often isn't a perfect method.

'I've been separated for four months now. We had a difficult time coming to an agreement about the children's care and we've now finally agreed on a shared arrangement, which seems to be going along quite well. However, lately I've been having some trouble with David, my ten-year-old son. He seems to have become quite belligerent with me, wanting to challenge me on everything and refusing to do as he's asked. I find it very trying

and last week I exploded and got very cross with him. What do
you think his behaviour means and how should I deal with it?'

First, we'll as usual try to understand what may be going on
— the context of your child's behaviour and the feelings
associated with his position. His parents have recently separated, so understandably he may be angry about it. If he thinks
you left his father and his father is sad and angry, he may know
this and be angry with you because his father is angry. At ten
years old a boy is very much needing to identify with his father
to develop a sense of his own emerging masculinity. In any
family this can lead to the appearance of apparently uncharacteristic oppositional behaviour which is sometimes very hard
for mums to deal with. They can easily become worn down
and emotional, feeling they've lost their authority.

What is often happening is that the boy is starting to feel he
needs to reject a lot of what he's been enjoying, such as warmth,
softness, nurturing and closeness, because they are feminine
things and they come from you, in order to become masculine
himself. This can express itself in quite strident rejection of
your authority while he is still too young to understand or
manage his emotional self. (We talked about the process of
individuation in Chapter 3.)

In your case something that is a normal developmental
process may have got mixed up with some separation-related
feelings and caught you at a time when (as we've said before)
your confidence in your parenting is affected. And apart from
probably feeling angry, David is having to make his own
adjustments to a new situation. Boys do tend to express inner
conflicts through aggression. Give him time, don't give in to
him, use all the listening and empathising skills you've learned
and be strong about setting limits on unacceptable behaviour.
Don't worry too much about having exploded, your patience

had reached its limit, but do talk to him soon about that day, choosing a calm moment. Tell him why you got cross, in terms of his behaviour not his character, and tell him you regret your outburst. Then talk to him about anger and aggression and all the reasons why he may be finding the separation difficult to get used to. Tell him that you will not tolerate rudeness or disobedience and remind him what you expect from him, perhaps referring to some of his behaviour that day. And be patient generally, taking breaks when you can from the constancy of parenting!

Perhaps even harder than answering direct questions or dealing with specific events is knowing what line to take when you think your children are feeling a bit upset about some aspect of 'the situation' but can't express it. There may be times when children reflect on their circumstances and have feelings they can't understand or express. They may tell you about upsetting dreams, or be withdrawn and moody, or have mystifying minor illnesses. They seem to be distressed out of all proportion to what they're saying the problem is. You try to help them talk to you about what's happening to them, and don't seem to be able to get to the bottom of it. It's frustrating because you want to help without making too much of it, but you don't want to make it worse by pressing them to explore the real issue, or making them think you're interpreting their feelings for them and telling them how they should be.

'I've been worried lately that my eleven-year-old son is troubled about his family situation. He's an only child and although he's apparently been managing our shared parenting arrangements for some time now, he seems rather sullen and uncommunicative. He doesn't complain, but I think he needs to open up about it. Should I try to get him to talk to me?'

Choose a relaxed and peaceful moment to ask him gently about what you've noticed, and see what reaction you get. Reassure him that the feelings underlying behaviour are often confusing. Tell him it's all right if he feels like being uncommunicative or if he's confused. Give him a few helpful pointers about likely reasons for feeling upset in a way that shows you think it's quite acceptable to feel these things, it's nothing to be ashamed of, and that disturbing or confused feelings are part of life.

This may be enough to remind him that you understand and get him talking. Don't expect what he says to make much sense or even really to reflect what's going on in his heart. Be reassuring, supportive and calm. Demonstrate at other times that you're happy to discuss your feelings openly too. However, remember that if you're right and he is feeling churned up about someone important in his family, it may be impossible for him to talk about this to you because it's connected with his parents being separated. (Sometimes a close person outside the family can be a useful confidant.) He may just be sorting it all out in his own way in his own time. He may be struggling with feelings of disappointment in his father for leaving the marriage, he may be yearning for more time with his father and he doesn't know how to deal with this. Boys learn early on that many feelings are not 'manly' to express and he wants to cover them up. This is regrettable, but is still very much how our sons sense they're meant to behave.

'My son came back from his father's the other day and said, "I hate you, Mum". Could he have been picking up something from his dad? Should I just ignore him?'

Don't ignore him, but don't for a moment think he means it or show your hurt. You are a valuable target for your child's emotional expressions, even though some of them may be aggressive or hurtful. Your child may return to your care after a period with his dad and feel angry about his parents' separateness, or your part, as he at that moment sees it, in the fact of your separation. Alternatively, he may feel it's your fault that he doesn't spend more time with his dad, because his dad has said he'd like to see him more but that his mum won't let him. He may be picking up on Dad's sadness and wanting to blame you. His dad may be letting it be known that he blames you. He may feel momentarily insecure about you, having had a fun time with his dad he's not sure if you'll approve of, and wants to test you out.

Acknowledge to him that he seems angry, and explain how when people feel angry they often feel they hate someone or something. Explain that sometimes your feelings cause you to say destructive things you don't really mean. Give him an everyday example, maybe something you did when you were angry such as uttering a hateful curse at the parking police for booking you. This will show him you are not destroyed by his remark, but that you understand he needed to say it, although it isn't a kind or pleasant remark. You have accepted his position, and sowed the idea in his mind that saying you hate people isn't helpful. Children can behave in very self-centred ways, and it's not abnormal for a child to say 'I hate you' just because they aren't getting their own way. What they mean is 'I hate you not giving me what I want', which is different from 'I hate *you*!'.

Try to keep communicating with children in a way that includes discussion about emotional expression. It can help them accept and even begin to understand their own feelings if they can try to express them to someone they trust; not just feelings about separation matters either, but about everything. Many parents are afraid to talk about emotional issues, sensitive or not, and find it hard to do this in a calm and instructive way, so they avoid it altogether. As we've pointed out, children need parents to be able to give them emotional guidance and advice about feelings and relationships just as much as they need it about the educational, social and recreational parts of their lives. It's a great mistake to neglect this, but a rather frequent one.

Children should be allowed and encouraged to express their thoughts and feelings to their family. Remember, this is where they try out everything they're learning about. You can help them acknowledge, understand and contain their confused emotions and sometimes unnecessary anxieties in helpful and healthy ways. In your conversations, help them to name their feelings themselves, rather than naming them for them. Try to convey to them that all emotions are valuable, even the ones we think of as negative because they are difficult to handle safely. For example, anger makes you stand up for yourself and protect yourself. Fear is useful in the right context: it makes us get out of the water quickly when a shark siren sounds and helps us avoid taking silly risks. It is important to express sadness because it enables us to deal with unhappy events, move on from them and get on with our lives.

Key Points about Truth, Fault and Feelings

- Take care in communicating the 'truth' as you see it. Aim to strike a sensible midpoint between unhelpful secrecy and blame-placing detail. Check your motives for wanting your children to know things about who's to blame for what.

- Don't be misled into thinking that everything's fine with the children because they aren't saying or doing anything of concern, and so you needn't bother with information or explanations. They may be internalising their feelings. They probably *are* fine, but be proactive and do some talking so they're informed and see from you that it is OK to discuss family matters.

- Think of your children's position when they ask questions and be prepared to show you acknowledge that their other parent's position is different from yours, not wrong.

- When there's time, turn their questions into opportunities for useful dialogue about family issues and relationships, blame and truth, etc.

- Accept their strong feelings as real at the time and offer ways of managing them which help your children towards greater independence, such as asking them what they feel and helping them identify their emotions.

- Remember that difficult-to-manage, intense emotional expressions are part of growing up. They may be extremely trying, but they don't mean you're failing as a parent, and they're not always something to do with a separation issue.

- Accept that there are times when being a parent does involve covering up your own feelings and playing down some of the facts. In theory this means you're compromising the congruence or authenticity of your expressions, but this is often necessary to safeguard your child's self-esteem because your feelings are so closely associated with their other parent.

CHAPTER 8

GETTING THERE

By now you've well and truly got the idea of effective communicating as a two-way process, an *exchange* of ideas not an *issuing of instructions*. Even though we really know this in theory, family life is often about fast-paced, almost automatic, exchanges, unless we take time to really think before we react, as we saw in Chapter 1. As parents, we tend to do more talking to or at our children than we do listening. This is partly a habit from when our children were very young and we felt responsible not only for teaching them how to speak, but also for guiding their every move; partly a legacy from the days when authoritarian, strict, children-should-be-seen-and-not-heard parenting traditions were the norm; and partly because many of us set out as parents thinking that our goal is to produce children who behave in desirable and obliging ways, who give us no 'trouble' and therefore make us feel in charge and successful.

There's nothing like the emotions of a separation to make you one-eyed about what's really going on and blind to other people's point of view, because you're feeling extra protective of your children and you're busy trying to justify your own viewpoint. Also, the legacy of your separation can make you sensitive for years about family events and your children's behaviour. As we've seen, this makes communicating the right amount of emotional freedom to our children a lot harder to achieve. Early on in a separation your own feelings about your former partner can be difficult to distinguish from your children's feelings about them. Assuming your child feels the same as you do about your estranged partner can be very inhibiting to their comfort in relating to them. This especially seems to happen in relation to a child who has the same gender as you. It can result in unhealthy alliances developing between you and your children at the expense of their relations with their other parent. By now you should be becoming aware of this if you've been really honest with yourself in your reactions to what we've covered!

Children growing up

If we don't adjust our guiding input as our children grow, so we progressively enhance their sense of their own mastery by allowing them to be individuals, we'll have trouble when they are teenagers and they want to be themselves. This may seem obvious, but unless you look at the way you come across to them you may not realise that you're imposing your own controls and not being open-minded about alternatives. Teenagers want to become independent. Their developmental task is to work out what they think and feel about things in their own right. This often involves a lot of alarming and perplexing experimentation which results in confrontations and arguments in families as parents try to retain some control and give the right kind of guidance. In any human relationship between two people who care for each other and have minds of their own there will be disagreements. It's why and how you disagree that matters, not that you do.

Teenagers need to feel listened to and that disagreements can be negotiated with everyone's point of view taken into account. They need to feel you respect them for having opinions which may be valid regardless of whether you agree with them. If you convey this they are much more likely to respect yours. You're unlikely to 'win' with your teenager if you always try to have the last word; instead, you'll have endless arguments and probably end up feeling you've lost any influence over them. You'll have joined the band of parents tearing their hair out over their uncontrollable, disrespectful young people! Teenagers need to assert their independence by reacting to authority and to experience the consequences of having responsibility for their own decisions. Negotiated compromise where both of you make some concessions is far more likely to work than insisting you have the last word. A willingness to compromise and be flexible is necessary on your part, if you are to expect this from your teenager too. Make sure you find time to listen. They may seem grown-up, independent and hardly ever at home, but they still need an approachable and interested family.

Integrating what you've learned

If you've got this far in this book you're well on your way to applying its principles in your own family relationships. Hopefully, you learned something useful from doing the self-rating exercise in Chapter 1 on how you communicate; and thought about the various points we covered about communication, and the goals for effective parenting and successful family life. Having learned more about how you communicate, especially in the heat of the moment when your feelings are aroused protectively, defensively, tearfully, etc., you now have a better idea of how to field your children's separation-related behaviour.

Unfortunately, insight and analysis don't in themselves bring about automatic changes in behaviour, although without them no progress is possible. Now you also have to do some serious and systematic practice in order to be able eventually to integrate permanent changes into the way you relate to your children. So, we'll take a look at what's involved in actually making real changes. Self-improvement through the acquisition of a new skill involves a series of steps:

- Define your *goal*.

- Identify what you want to change and your *target behaviours*, and work out what habits, attitudes and emotional blockages tend to govern how you're currently performing. In other words, establish your *baseline*.

- Find out what situations are most likely to trigger your current way of performing, your *danger zones* if you like!

- Inform yourself of the *strategies* you know you want to put in place, instead of your habitual ones, in order to achieve your overall goal.

- *Practise* these strategies or techniques in easier situations, gradually progressing towards applying them in harder ones.

- Keep going with your practice, expecting *gradual success*, and don't be too hard on yourself when you don't get a perfect score.

- You'll arrive at the point where you feel most of the time you've got there! Your new skill is in place and mostly automatic or *integrated* now.

These are the steps you need to progress through in order to convert insight into real change. Now we'll translate these steps to fit your task — the one that made you want to read this book — to help you on your self-improvement journey.

- Your *goal* is to help your children with their divided family by improving your communication skills.

- Your *target behaviours* are your honest answers to the self-rating checklist in Chapter 1, which might include: I tend to answer for my children, cutting off opportunities for them to think and speak for themselves; I tend to give in and try to 'rescue' my children because I feel responsible and protective; I tend to avoid talking about sensitive topics, etc.

- Your *danger zones* are situations which you know undermine your performance as a communicator, for example, hearing things you disapprove of about how your ex-partner deals with your children; when people criticise you, you feel threatened; you raise your voice when you're angry; you give in on limit-setting to compensate for inflicting a separation on your children, etc.

- You know about the importance of listening; seeking clarification; inviting your child to say what they think and feel; working out solutions together rather than imposing yours; showing open-minded understanding; being sufficiently honest about family realities; avoiding sending messages that invite your children to take sides, etc.; and all the many other communication tools we've described. These are your *strategies*.

- *Practise* your new skills of listening attentively, checking what the speaker really said before you respond, using self-responsible 'I' language, etc., in a relatively calm situation, like doing a school project together or having family discussion at a mealtime. Have some fun just as a couple, trying out your new methods, and ask for your partner's impressions!

- Analyse your attempts after the event in your own mind, noting what you said and how you said it. See if there's room for further improvement. Be willing to avoid certain situations that you know are difficult while you give yourself more time for *gradual progress* in adjusting to all the potentially disruptive emotions caused by a separation in your past.

- Keep going and you'll start to notice your children responding favourably. Your new skills will begin to become *integrated* into the way you communicate.

You'll also start to notice a satisfying feeling of empowerment, because you've put your mind to doing something important and gone a long way towards achieving it. You'll also find that taking action about something helps you detach from unhelpful attitudes and emotional blockages, many of which probably relate to your ongoing disappointment in your ex-partner, both as a partner to you, and as a parent. You will have changed your attitude, which will help you keep your behavioural changes in place and really integrate them.

Don't for a moment think that any of this is easy to do; feelings always tend to interfere with performance. Real application is required to manage these feelings more effectively.

Revisiting some key issues

Being a parent under any circumstances is a challenge, but because most of us *are* parents we tend to see it as something that just happens. Instinct is therefore supposed to take care of the challenges. The challenges *are* normal, but they're still real and need to be faced head-on. Anticipating the negative aspects of inevitable realities, and being ready for them, is, in fact, being positive. Some of us don't approach them very realistically, because we think that having children is such a usual thing for everyone that somehow we're meant to know how to do it. This makes it harder for us to admit that adjustments have to be made and effort put in, and that we can get it wrong, affecting how our children turn out, perhaps disadvantaging them. Most families are nothing like the happy, cooperative, problem-free, accomplished group we set out to create. We tend to have idealised models of happy family life, but don't know what steps to take to construct one actively. You can't change the fact that family life with a past can sometimes be sad, hectic, confusing, disappointing, and enraging; but then so can life in general sometimes.

We don't usually question the love we have and are always meant to feel for our children. But they are separate beings and so are bound to disappoint us sometimes, or even seem unlovable. Lots of what children say and do is impulsive, reflects confused motives, is manipulative, spontaneous, completely insignificant or downright annoying. Your patience may be on trial, but remember that children need to emote randomly as they slowly learn about their ability to impact on the world and understand their feelings. However, they also need your guidance in learning to consider others and experience the consequences of their behaviour.

Your children are not an extension of you, they are individuals. They are a complex mixture of what they happened to be born like (part of which is inherited from you), and the combined effects of all they experience from the moment of conception onwards. You and your feelings are separate from your children and their feelings, and they need to be. After a separation you may find yourself wanting to attribute aspects of your children's make-up that you don't like to those parts of their experience that their other parent (your ex-partner) is responsible for. Accept these feelings in yourself but don't convey them to your children personally. As we've seen, they need to believe you approve of them, although they must know that you can't approve of all they do.

You're probably very ready to worry that your child is expressing something about this thing — having separated — that you inflicted upon them and that you feel very responsible for; or that their behaviour reflects some irritation you have about your ex-partner, which is adult divorce baggage. This makes you supersensitive and inclined to think you've got to deal with every expression your child makes that's even remotely connected to a possible separation factor. We've shown how you should check you're not worrying unduly by taking a step back and looking at the context within which your child is functioning, and considering alternative meanings for their behaviour which may have nothing to do with the separation factor. We've also cautioned against taking children's remarks too literally, and advised you stop and think before assuming what they mean. In this liberal, children-should-be-heard age we can attribute a greater maturity and validity to their expressions than they are capable of really handling.

When you want to respond or feel you have to intervene, remember there often isn't a perfect response or way of handling things. Try to remember the guiding principles: attend to your child, listen accurately, never take sides, find a way to validate your child's emotional reality in your response, make further inquiries, help them describe their position and feelings, and suggest some neutral interpretations referring to human nature in general and individual differences in the way people handle things. Keep your dialogue light-hearted but open and confident-sounding.

When you're not sure how to respond, do what counsellors (for different reasons) do: ask for more information, taking the comment further, with questions like 'How did that make you feel?', 'What did you do?', 'What happened then?', etc. This gives you time, extends the conversation so you get more information to go on, and makes you seem interested and tells your child you have time for them. Give them some gentle suggestions, without telling them what you think they must feel or should have done; for example, 'When someone feels angry and cross, they feel like hitting back, but that often doesn't seem to help' or 'When you feel hurt, sometimes you want to crawl into a hole by yourself and be miserable!'. That way they know you understand, but you've responded in terms of human nature and its complexities in general, rather than telling them how to be. You can tell children about situations you've found difficult yourself (not ones directly to do with them, of course) and how you resolved them, including things you did that you regret with hindsight.

Here are some more ideas for lines you might use to help you keep conversations open, light-hearted, blame-free and instructive when children comment on another adult's behaviour:

- *'Maybe he got out of bed the wrong side this morning!'* This offers a low-key reason for someone's mood, normalising fluctuations in people's frame of mind and placing responsibility with that person rather than with the child.

- *'Maybe she's got something else on her mind.'* This suggests a reason for a person's preoccupation and apparent lack of attention in terms of her own possible position, rather than the child's value to her, without passing judgment.

- *'Sometimes people sound short and we take it personally when it's not about us at all.'* Here's a response that offers an alternative reason for crankiness other than that the child has caused it, which gives a child something helpful to think about rather than taking on responsibility for it themself.

- *'I don't like it either when Mum gets cranky like that, but never mind.'* This shows an adult can share and thus support another person's feelings without showing it gets to him, which offers a child a model for taking minor outbursts in their stride.

- *'Maybe you feel upset because we can't all be together anymore. I can understand that.'* This expresses recognition that aspects of the child's position require some adjustments that you're aware of, and is reassuring.

- *'What do you think Dad might have meant when he said that?'* This offers the child the opportunity to form their own idea of what was meant before interpreting the remark for them, and avoids making a judgment while more information is sought about how the child feels.

- *'Do you have any ideas about what you could do about that?'* Here the child is offered the opportunity to think about a solution of their own.

- *'Do you remember that time I got really cross because the car wouldn't start? I think I kicked the front tyre or something, but it didn't really help, did it?'* Showing you have experienced irritation helps a child to feel they can express theirs, while you point out that aggression results from anger, though it doesn't usually solve anything.

- *'Maybe you could try to explain that to Dad next time, so he knows how you feel.'* This conveys that you aren't responsible for your child's relationship with their other parent, though you're interested in helping them work things out for themself.

These are just some more suggestions to get you thinking. They're not necessarily the perfect lines, but they're designed to get you started generating your own repertoire of alternatives to rushing in with protective responses to communications you're inclined to react sensitively to because they concern your child's other parent.

When you have afterthoughts or regrets about conversations where you think you could have done better, you can have reruns later which help towards resolution and can usefully prevent a child internalising inaccurate interpretations which arose because of realities that weren't expressed, information that was withheld, or tensions that interfered with accurate listening. You're only human, and if you think you handled something harshly, open the topic again and have another discussion, or use it to add your potentially helpful afterthoughts. Another advantage of reruns is that at the time the child may be too wound up to listen rationally. Choose a calm moment, and then recent conflicts can often be resolved rather than being swept under the carpet and supposedly forgotten.

Set some guidelines for family communication. Incorporate regular family discussions where everyone is free to have a say, have their viewpoints listened to, but in such a way that you (and your partner) remain in charge of decisions about how something is going to be handled while listening empathically to everyone's point of view. Try to reach some sort of consensus that incorporates teenagers' needs for independence, if older children are involved: see above. Remember the importance of parental authority, discussed in Chapter 6.

Partnership-power

Don't forget the importance of communication between adults about children and family policy. This is essential between you and your current partner as heads of your stepfamily. Ideally, it should be able to happen between you and your ex-partner about your own natural children who share two homes, as important decisions like schooling or changing the shared parenting arrangements arise. As parents of children who belong to two households, you may well have two partnerships to look after, one present and one past but now different.

Setting aside time to discuss things — and not necessarily just about the children — is often neglected until there's a particular problem. Try being proactive rather than reactive; it'll be good for your relationship and this has positive spin-offs for the children. To help you get started we'll look at some ground rules for constructive discussion. This may seem contrived, but new methods do tend to feel awkward at first and having a structure often helps, even though it may seem a bit artificial and effortful. Sensitive and personal topics are often neglected for fear of the emotional responses that may be triggered if they're discussed. Yet often they're the most important things to address. Setting some rules makes discussion seem less threatening. We often don't think of applying the established and helpful methods at home that we use for meetings outside the family, like appointing a chairperson, having a time limit or an agenda. You can use them constructively in families without being overly formal.

- Limit the time you're going to spend on the topic at one sitting, and keep the 'agenda' a realistic length.

- Undertake to listen and repeat what you hear the other say to check for misunderstandings, before making assumptions about apparent meanings and intentions.

- Agree that you won't dredge up the past and that you'll behave as if each has the unquestionable right to their point of view (you don't have to agree with it, but you don't have to be right either!).

- Permit each other not to know what you think about a particular topic or point of view, and seek time for thought and inquiry. Family stuff is often confusing and uncertain, because it's sensitive and personal.

- Allow statements or opinions to be provisional and able to be reopened, modified or added to.

- Before closing the discussion, sum up your positions and/or the agreed action clearly and note what topics are to be continued at another time.

- If either of you wants to conclude the discussion before the other, accept this but also acknowledge it clearly. For example, one of you might be getting angry or upset and know you're getting near your 'danger zone' for showing it.

So you should say: 'I don't think we're getting anywhere on this, I'm finding it frustrating so I'd like to finish. Let's make time to try again'. This is better than stopping abruptly and unilaterally. Always try to note together where the discussion has been left.

- You can apply these principles to having family conferences at home involving everyone, including the family pet! Sensitive issues come up in stepfamilies, as we've seen, and difficult discussions aren't confined to meetings you need to have with your ex-partner. Make a special effort to establish good communication in your new partnership so you avoid some of the difficulties you had in your last one.

Parent-care

Don't neglect yourself in your efforts to be a super-communicating parent. Self-reflection and looking after your own interests is not necessarily the same as being self-indulgent. Think of time out from children and family responsibilities as a well-deserved and necessary recharging of your batteries. Putting other people first all the time, something that committed parents, especially homemaking mothers, quite often do, can sometimes make you feel frustrated, resentful, unappreciated or unfulfilled. You probably won't show it (or won't think you do), perhaps because you think these feelings aren't very admirable and should be suppressed, or you aren't aware of what it is that's making you feel that your life or your partnership isn't quite working out for you.

You have an existence in your own right, outside of your role as a parent, and you should attend to this part of you even though family life is so important and at times all-consuming.

Cultivate that part of you that existed before you became a partner and a parent, and find some kind of outlet for its expression. Make time for a neglected interest that gives you links with life outside 'home and hearth'. Fathers often have a more ready arena for self-expression and creativity outside of marriage and family life in their world of work. Young families often require one parent to go without this opportunity for some time. If this is you, don't neglect friendships and personal interests entirely in favour of parenting and partnership responsibilities, but take care to avoid overload. Everyone's emotional health depends on nurturing their own self independently of their relationship with others who are dependent on them. And your children need to feel you have an identity of your own with your own interests and enthusiasms, so you convey to them by your own example that they are free to develop their own characters as well as being your children.

So make sure you put yourself first sometimes, exploring the individual creativity and potential that's inside you somewhere, including your talent for parenting. A good counsellor can help you explore and extend yourself in positive ways, as well as help you get over a relationship that may still be affecting you more than you'd like it to; also, just like talking to a trusted and patient friend, you can let your hair down and forget about all your efforts at more effective communication for a while! Looking after yourself needn't mean you neglect anybody else. It can mean a more contented you, less governed by other people and circumstances, with more to offer others, especially your children.

There's no such thing as a perfect score in parenting. Feeling guilty about how you're managing is much less helpful than confiding in a partner or friend and resolving to have another crack at it next time. Try to think of your goals for improved communication as long-term ones. You need to persevere and forget about the idea of a quick fix. Parenting is for the long haul so your continued efforts won't be wasted. Also, your communication with others in all walks of life will be more satisfying and productive.

FINALE

Let's hope your divorce can become a happy ending of a kind after all. It's what spurred you to become an even better parent by prompting you to look at family life, and communication in particular, in more detail than you would have otherwise. Let's hope you can now give yourself a great score on listening to your children as well as having them listen to you. Your listening skills have made you into an approachable parent, which we'd all like to be, especially during our children's teenage years.

Making time to talk, having real conversations as a family, not just communicating on the run, helps children feel that their family is a solid anchor from which to make their excursions into independent life, and that home is a place where there's always someone interested in them and who has time for them. Unhurried mealtimes are a great opportunity for reinforcing the family as a unit through enjoying just conversing together.

Being able to promptly take a mental step back and ask 'what's really going on here?' will make your responses more empathic and understanding.

Being aware of your weak points so you can put in place better ways to manage them will make you more in charge of your emotional self.

Transmitting attentive authority when appropriate, but increasingly allowing freedom for your children to make their own decisions and mistakes as they grow older, will help them become independent individuals.

Skilfully avoiding apportioning blame in such a way that you don't endorse things you disapprove of by saying nothing, means you convey open-mindedness and give children freedom to form their own opinions and have their own relationships with important people. Remember the 'everyone's different' or the 'maybe they were feeling cranky' lines, to help you with this.

Being prepared to review your communication behaviour regularly, asking trusted friends and partners for feedback, and exploring resources on communication strategies and parenting skills will help you stay 'on line'.

SUGGESTED FURTHER READING

Here are some publications which take many of the topics covered further. Their titles are self-explanatory.

Balson, Maurice, *Becoming Better Parents*, The Australian Council for Educational Research, Melbourne, 1991.

Biddulph, Steve, *The Secret of Happy Children*, Bay Books, HarperCollins, Sydney, 1994.

Burrett, Jill, *To and Fro Children: A guide to successful parenting after divorce*, Allen & Unwin, Sydney, 1991.

Burrett, Jill, *Dad's Place: A new guide for fathers after divorce*, Angus and Robertson, HarperCollins, Sydney, 1996.

Glennon, Will, *Fathering: Strengthening connection with your children no matter where they are*, Conari Press, California, 1995.

Gottman, John, *The Heart of Parenting: How to raise an emotionally intelligent child*, Bloomsbury Publishing, London, 1997.

Hart-Byers, Sue, *Secrets of Successful Stepfamilies*, Lothian, Melbourne, 1998.

Hayman, Suzie, *You Just Don't Listen: A parent's guide to improving communication with young people*, Vermilion, London, 1998.

Mackay, Hugh, *The Good Listener: Better relationships through communication*, Macmillan, Sydney, 1998.

Mulvaney, Alison, *Talking With Kids: How to improve communication — and your relationship — with your children*, Simon & Schuster Australia, Sydney, 1995.

Tannen, Deborah, *You Just Don't Understand: Women and men in conversation*, Virago Press, London, 1990.

USEFUL AGENCIES

Australian Council For Educational Research Publishes multimedia products on all aspects of parenting and education. They are based in Melbourne. Tel: (03) 9277 5555. Address: 19 Prospect Hill Road, Camberwell; Private Bag 55, Camberwell Victoria 3124.

Australian Psychological Society This is the professional organisation of practising psychologists. They have a database of licensed psychologists which you can consult for names of local practitioners specialising in relationship, child and family counselling. They are based in Melbourne. Tel: (toll-free) 1800 333 497. Address: 1 Grattan Street, Carlton; PO Box 126, Carlton South Victoria 3053.

Department of Community Services Each state has a government department equivalent to the New South Wales Department of Community Services. They provide information and support services for parents and families. Consult your white pages for local details.

Family Court of Australia This is a Federal Government facility which exists to help families in conflict about separation issues. It has substantial counselling and mediation services to encourage out-of-court private dispute resolution, and some branches offer confidential counselling and information services, as well as parenting courses. Branches in major population centres. Listed in the white pages under Commonwealth Government Agencies.

Interrelate Formerly known as the Family Life Movement, this Federal Government-funded agency, whose national head office is in Sydney (tel: (02) 9747 6700), offers relationship, family and personal counselling, and parenting advice and courses. Contact the head office or see your white pages for local details.

Relationships Australia Formerly the Marriage Guidance Council, this is another Federal Government-funded agency offering relationship counselling, parenting and family advice and courses. Branches in most major cities. Contact national head office in Canberra (tel: (02) 6285 4466) or your local office (see your white pages for details).

INDEX